"Hard Work

FLASHBACKS NO.2

The Flashback series is sponsored by the
European Ethnological Research Centre,
c/o the National Museums of Scotland,
Queen Street, Edinburgh EH2 1JD.

General Editor: Alexander Fenton

"HARD WORK, YE KEN"

Midlothian Women Farm Workers

Ian MacDougall

TUCKWELL PRESS
in association with
Midlothian District Council
The European Ethnological Research Centre and
The National Museums of Scotland, Edinburgh

First published in Great Britain in 1993
by Canongate Academic

Reprinted in 1996 by
Tuckwell Press Ltd
The Mill House
Phantassie
East Linton, East Lothian EH40 3DG
Scotland

© Midlothian District Council
ISBN 1 898410 05 4

Cataloguing-in-publication Data:
A catalogue record for this book is available
on request from the British Library

Typeset by Hewer Text
Printed by Cromwell Press, Melksham, Wilts

Contents

Foreword

It is an important part of our attitude to history at the present time that the knowledge of ordinary folk—that is, most of us—is being taken into account. There is an upsurge in the recording of oral history. At the opposite end of the country from Midlothian, in Orkney, a volume was recently published on *Old Orkney Trades* (ed. Sheila Spence, The Orkney Press, 1988), covering the work of a road-metaller, well-borer, stonemason, quarryman, wheelwright, shoemaker, and one woman, a tailoress. The present volume, concentrating on the work of women farm workers, brings a further dimension to the oral history scene.

The four women present their own experience, in their own words, with dialect expressions and phrases characteristic of Midlothian, in a natural, unforced way that makes the reader feel as if he were listening to the spoken word. They present in each case a complete experience. We are given details not only of the work done, but also of home life, families, dress, food and entertainment.

Time and again we are made aware of the nature of country folk who tolerated hard work, long hours and tiredness, but were still able to speak up for themselves smartly enough if the farmer overdid things. We hear of the Farm Servants' Union (of which the founding conference took place in June 1912 in Turriff, Aberdeenshire) which certainly helped to improve conditions, though marginally enough at first by snipping a fraction off twelve-hour days and establishing a half-day on Saturdays. But the Union's growth was probably held back by the generally phlegmatic and little-complaining attitude of farm workers, male as well as female.

As one brought up in the Turriff district in a crofting and small farming community at a period also covered in the present book, I was vividly reminded time and again of details that were once part of my own daily life. At the same time, I was mentally engaged, as readers from other areas will be, by the range of differences, stemming largely from the larger scale of farming activities in Midlothian. In the days of horse-power, farmers needed bondagers on the work force, they had to have extra seasonal labour from the neighbouring villages and towns and from Ireland, if the major tasks of the year, above all the grain and potato harvests, were to be handled with the necessary speed. Midlothian made far more use of women than many other parts of Scotland, and this must be seen as one of the characteristics of Midlothian farming up to and for some time after the adoption of the tractor and other modern technology. Another point of some interest is the alternation of farm work and mining (at least for male members of the family).

One of the contributors, a Dalkeith girl, spent much of her working life amongst the tatties, being employed by a potato merchant, and technically, therefore, she is a farm worker. At the same time her town background allows her to provide much insight into the life of a Midlothian town, including the importance of the pawn shop in the weekly struggle for food, the lodging houses that catered for immigrant workers, the town dairies with their byres, and the excitement of surreptitiously laying hold of one of the boss's hens or an extra pocketful of potatoes.

Amongst the many interesting aspects of these reminiscences are the details given of food and meal times, which, of course, tie in with the daily work cycle. The conserving of boiled meat in jars sealed with mutton fat is an old technique. Ewe's milk cheese kept on being made until well through the century, a fact which may surprise many historians. But whilst the contributors living in the country ate relatively well, tea, bread and jam were much more the standard diet of the Dalkeith lass.

Oral history of this kind has to be read slowly and absorbed well, for it is a distillation of long experience. No one can ever know an individual's life and background better than that individual. The patient accumulation of such information for Midlothian, as for other parts of Scotland, will undoubtedly bring, through the knowledge gained, fresh perspectives on the history of our districts and regions.

Reference numbers in the plate section refer to negatives in the Scottish Ethnological Archive, National Museums of Scotland.

Alexander Fenton

Introduction

Midlothian has lain so long in the southern shadow of that great capital city Edinburgh that it remains arguably one of the lesser-known areas of Scotland. The aim of this little book is to help make Midlothian, and its people, better known. It is hoped this may prove the first in a series of presentations of the oral history of the district.

Midlothian has many places of natural beauty and historical and architectural interest—among others, Roslin Chapel, the Pentland Hills, Vogrie Estate Country Park, the valleys of the rivers North and South Esk, and Borthwick, Crichton and Dalhousie Castles.

But one of the great attractions of Midlothian, as of so many other parts of Scotland, is surely its people. Their experience of work and life is a microcosm of much of Scotland's heritage, especially its industrial heritage.

Here four women tell us of their experiences working on the land. Two of them, Mrs Lindsay and the late Mrs Tod who died in 1988, recall working and living conditions before the First World War. The working experience of the two other women, Mrs Landells and Mrs Walker, was first gained between the two World Wars and then continued during and since 1945.

All four women speak straight from their own experience. Their oral history is a living testimony of what it was like for women to work in all weathers out in the fields, ploughing or harvesting, milking cows and tending cattle, hoeing turnips or howking and pitting tatties. And besides working conditions, wages and hours of labour, their recollections embrace a variety of other aspects of social and economic history, such as housing, diet, recreation, hiring fairs, the pawn shop, Irish seasonal workers and the impact on local families of the 1914–18 War.

An effort has been made throughout to preserve and present the actual words of these four women farm workers as they recall their experiences. Editing has involved chiefly the exclusion of repetitious matter, and some transpositions have been made to secure a more coherent presentation. Each of the four women kindly checked and approved her own text.

To Midlothian District Council thanks are due for authorising and encouraging the undertaking of this publication. Thanks are also due for particular help given by Councillors Dick Small and David Smith, the late Mr William Sked, former Depute Director of Administration, Mr Alan Reid, District Librarian, and his predecessor Mr Brian Osborne, Miss Marion Richardson, Local Studies Librarian, as well as to Mrs Betty Grandison for patient typing of transcripts and drafts. Professor Sandy Fenton has persevered undaunted by the recession in his quest for a publisher for these recollections—and in Canongate Academic and Mr John Tuckwell he has found a particularly sympathetic one. Above all, thanks are due to Mrs Lindsay, Mrs Landells, Mrs Walker and the late Mrs Tod for allowing me to interview them and record their experiences.

Ian MacDougall
Public Relations Officer
Midlothian District Council

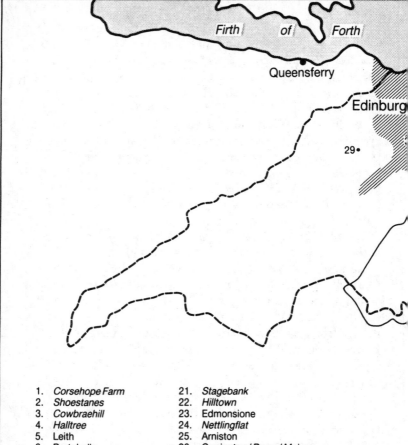

Firth of Forth

Queensferry

Edinburg

29•

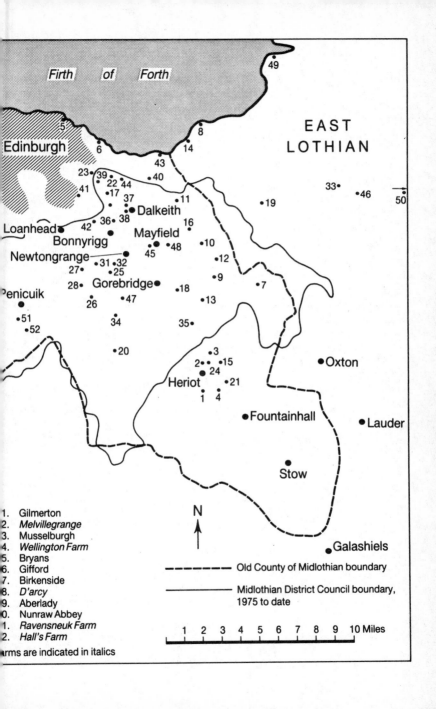

Firth of Forth

EAST LOTHIAN

Edinburgh

Loanhead

Bonnyrigg

Newtongrange

Penicuik

Dalkeith

Mayfield

Gorebridge

Heriot

Oxton

Lauder

Fountainhall

Stow

Galashiels

49
5
6
8
14
43
23 39
40
33
46
50
22 44
41 17
37
11
19
42 36 38
16
10
45 48
12
27 31 32
9
7
25
28
18
26 47
13
34
35
20
3
2 15
24
1 4 21

1. Gilmerton
2. *Melvillegrange*
3. Musselburgh
4. *Wellington Farm*
5. Bryans
6. Gifford
7. Birkenside
8. *D'arcy*
9. Aberlady
10. Nunraw Abbey
11. *Ravensneuk Farm*
12. *Hall's Farm*

arms are indicated in italics

N

———— Old County of Midlothian boundary

———— Midlothian District Council boundary, 1975 to date

1 2 3 4 5 6 7 8 9 10 Miles

Mrs Agnes Tod

I was born on the 17th of August 1895 at Corsehope farm, near Heriot, in the old county of Midlothian. My father was a ploughman at Corsehope.

It was a very big farm—oh, into the thousand acres – but there was not much arable. My father wasn't the only ploughman—there was another man, a young lad—but there were two shepherds. I can remember the names of the shepherds: Andrew Redpath, who lived next door to my father, was one, but he was away before I was born. And then there was John Blake.

I think the shepherds were better paid. Of course, they had a seven-day-a-week job and they were responsible for all the stock. To me the shepherds seemed to be a different breed: they were on that side and the men that did the real work was on the other. I think they thought they were a wee bit better than the ordinary farm worker, a step above the ploughmen. I don't know if that was because they thought they were more skilled or better paid. They just lived next door to us in the same sort o' house. They were all good neighbours, there was no standing back from the ploughmen; in fact, the shepherds' wives and the ploughmen's wives were just like sisters.[1]

When I was born in 1895 there would be about 1,500 or 1,600 sheep on Corsehope farm. They were breeding

I

ewes, so there were lambs in addition, and tups and rams as well. The best lambs were kept and the other lambs—what we called the ordinary lambs—they were castrated and fed fat for sale.

My father was born in or about 1856. I remember he was eighty when he died in 1936. I was seventh in our family. I had six brothers and four sisters, and there was one twin boy who had died in infancy. I had three brothers and three sisters older than me and three brothers and a sister younger. We were all born at home, every one of us.

I mind o' being taken by my mother to see my grandfather—father's father—just before he died. He worked on the farm all his life at Oxton, near Lauder in Berwickshire. He was a ploughman. Sandy Douglas was his name. He was born at Netherhowden at Oxton and worked there practically all his working life. He was only sixty-eight when he died, and that was when I was just three, so he must have been born about 1830.

Grandfather Douglas was always a ploughman. I think in harvest—the busy times—they worked from daylight till dark. And there was no overtime or anything like that in those days. His wage was eighteen shillings a week because he was foreman and looked after the place. And then the next man had two shillings less, and the boys—young strong boys—had just about ten shillings a week.

Grandfather had retired, through illness, I think, three years before he died. I suppose he was worked done. It was very hard work in those days. There was no fork lifts or anything. Horses was grandfather's life.

Grandmother Douglas died young. She was a publican's daughter. Her parents had Jock's Lodge pub at

Piershill in Edinburgh. But they had a country house in Lauder and they came there for summer holidays and she met my grandfather and married him. Her people disowned her because she married a ploughman. They would have no more to do with her. But they came to see her when her first child was nine. They took him away for a holiday—but they kept him. She never got him back. Oh, it wasn't done by agreement. In those days people just did what they liked. They just took her eldest child away and kept him. But I'm not sure she would be broken-hearted: I suppose she had so many more she'd be hoping they'd take another one!

Well, when that eldest son grew up he was left his grandparents' business. He married and his wife drank him out of business and then he started working with horse-drawn lorries in Edinburgh. He used to come tae us for holidays after his wife died. A right old nuisance he was!

We didn't hear any more about grandmother Douglas' parents. They wouldn't have anything to do with us, we were farm folks, you see. Grandmother was an only child, Ellen Fraser was her name. I can't remember ever seeing her. But they were just all hard-working people and quite content with their lot as far as ever I heard.

When I was four years old we left Corsehope farm and went to another farm called Shoestanes, just above Heriot and quite near the railway station. My father was the foreman or grieve there too. In fact, he was the only ploughman there, the only man on that place, him and my brother, but of course my brother was just a boy. But he would work wi' horses and do all the things that was required.

We stayed in that farm with father three years and

then he moved over to the other side of the railway to Cowbraehill. That's a wee bit away from Heriot, at Tynehead. That was in 1902. We were at Cowbraehill six years and then we went to Halltree. That's between Heriot and Fountainhall, on the way south but still in the county of Midlothian. I think father was at Halltree four years. As the boys grew up he had to shift to get work for them. That was very important, because he wanted to keep them at home! He just liked having them at home, I think it would be that he could keep an eye on them. However, they went away one by one and got into other jobs.

We were never what they called badly off. Of course we were always dressed in home-made dresses. My mother made them all. They were generally hand-me-downs from somebody that gave mother dresses and she took the good bits and made dresses for us. Sometimes they were much better than cotton, maybe velvet or something like that, whatever she could get.

It was friends from the town that gave mother dresses, maybe a cousin working to somebody in a house and the lady of that house would give her the stuff. My mother was a dressmaker so she always got the things to make down. She had an old treadle sewing machine. She worked at it quite a lot, making our clothes. She made clothes for other people too, just for a few shillings, I suppose. It was a small income for herself. I can remember her making a sunshade for the window of the sweetie shop. She took me with her when she took the shade home. The sunshade was made from a sort of canvas, a heavy material. It was a big heavy job.

If she was making a dress and wanted to finish it or making underwear she worked sometimes on till two in the morning. She did the sewing after we were all in bed.

And then she got flour bags from a baker and she bleached them and made underwear for us for the summer. They were very comfortable to wear. We didn't feel embarrassed at having to wear flour bags, oh, no, we were very proud of them because mother had put so much work on them. People like us, we were lucky because we had a mother wi' clever hands. We were better off than some other farm workers' children because mother was so well doing. They didn't have all those things. She could make things for us. We never went about with worn or dirty clothes. She was an excellent mother.

And we were never hungry. My father always kept pigs and they were killed for consumption in the home. He kept two at a time and then we always had maybe two dozen or so hens. So we could have all sorts of food—hen and chicken soup and the meat minced up and made into patties or something like that to spread over the big family. When a hen had laid her lauchter—that meant when she had laid for maybe three years and then began laying small eggs—she was ready for the pot.[2] Then my mother used to boil a hen and a piece of the home-cured ham, and fill jars wi' that and seal them with mutton fat, so that if anybody came there was no shortage of a sandwich. We always had plenty of visitors.

At breakfast time, well, my father got up at a quarter to five and the others had to get up shortly after that, and they got a cup of tea and butter and bread. Then my mother took ham and egg and put that into scones at eight o'clock and took that out to the field for father and my brothers. When we were going to school we got ham and egg and fried bread every morning before we went. We had to be well fed—we had a long way to go to school.

We got porridge once a day, at five o'clock when they came in for the evening meal. Father didn't like porridge in the morning—and in our house we all turned when father turned!

We always had our own cow and the butter we ate was home-made. Our cow was kept in the byre with the farmer's cow. You paid the farmer three shillings and sixpence a week for the cow's keep. It was just the foreman ploughman that kept a cow; I don't think the other ploughmen were interested.

I never was very fond of milk, never. But of course my mother baked bread, scones and bannocks. And she baked pease bannocks to take with soup. It was pease dried and ground at the mill and then you bought the meal from the shop and with soup it was very good. It was a brown coarse bread but very, very tasty.

We went out to the woods and gathered wild rasps and gooseberries. That was what we did on Saturdays and in the evening after we came from school. There were very few people that did it where we were but we were told to do it—and we did what we were told! Mother would just say, "Now hurry up wi' your tea and you will go and get some rasps." And my two brothers and I would go away and my sisters older than me, and we would bring back pitchers o' rasps and then mother made them into jam. She also bought strawberries and made jam, and my grandfather had plenty fruit so we used to go and pull raspberries there too. So we always had plenty jam.

6

Mrs Agnes Tod

My mother always made marmalade to last through the year. That was in the month of February. She got Seville oranges and made the marmalade. And grandfather Denholm kept bees. He had a big garden. He had plenty of fruit. We were always quite near them.

When we gathered wild raspberries and gooseberries we got a saucerful each with some milk when we came in and then the rest was all made into jam. We ate oranges only at Christmas. Later on, when we were all working, we used to have them every week when the grocer came. My father thought that was a complete waste, buying oranges.

There were apple trees in the garden but they were old trees and the apples were sour. They were made into tarts and dumplings. We never had any dessert apples. When I would be about twelve or fourteen my eldest brother was working in Leith and when he came home at the weekend he would bring a melon and divide it among us all. So it was a very small piece we got. But every time he came he brought things for us.

We weren't familiar wi' bananas at all. We went once a year to Portobello for a day and then we would get bananas and things that we saw in the shops, but we didn't have them for a regular meal.

My mother also used to make ewe cheese. When the lambs were taken away from the ewes the shepherd brought them into the fold. Some o' the women went out in the morning and milked the ewes and made ewe cheese from that. It was a very soft white cheese but very good to eat and very good food, full of nourishment. You see, the ewes were grazing and getting all the minerals they needed.

Potatoes were very much an important part of our

diet. We got boiled potatoes, fried potatoes and stovie potatoes. Well, the stovies were a treat. If mother had a bit cold meat left over she'd put in the onion, potatoes and the cold meat on top and you got a plate of stovies and that was excellent.

Father was a very good gardener and grew all the vegetables. But he was allowed 1,600 yards in the field to grow potatoes. He had to provide the seed and the tattie pickers to lift them. So you had all those potatoes in a pit in the garden to see you through the winter. That was a lot of potatoes—almost a mile of potatoes. Of course, the pigs got the small ones and the tattie peelings. But father didn't sell any of the potatoes. He sometimes gave them away. My cousins in the town got a bag at lifting time and maybe if they happened to be going in any time through the year they would get a bag then too.

The potatoes was part of my father's wages, and quite a considerable part. Then that was stopped and they got one ton of potatoes for through the year each just from the field. I would be about ten when that started, round about 1905. I think it was changed because some of the people just didnae bother taking their ground, though my father did. My father liked the 1,600 yards. He could have his own seed. And he had always plenty of boys to go and gather them. Some people hadn't.

As for meat, apart from the pork and ham from the pig, we always had other meat on Sunday. Shoulder steak mother had on Sundays, and we used to get mince. We didnae have meat every day but on Sundays we always had an extraordinary dinner. Well, the men had time to eat it on a Sunday and then have a rest after.

As I say, mother baked brown bread and scones and

8

bannocks. But she was a good customer of the baker too. She paid him once a month and when she paid her monthly bill she would maybe get a cake from the baker and white loaves for toasting. And she would sometimes buy meat pies from the baker. The only time we had cakes was at Christmas: currant loaf (they call it black bun nowadays) and sultana cake.

The baker came wi' a horse and cart from Blackshiels village and then he got a motor van. Tom Clark was the name o' one o' the bakers. He came regularly twice a week and went round all the farm places. And he brought in other messages you wanted from the shop. If you just let the shopkeeper know that you wanted something—maybe at jam-making time he would bring a hundredweight sack of sugar—so that saved the grocer's vanman. He hadn't room in his van for hundredweights of sugar so the baker would bring them or maybe anything special that you wanted.

We got fish once a week. There was a man came on a bicycle at one time with two boxes of fish. Very few people bought them. I don't know why they didn't but my mother always did. The man must have come from East Lothian somewhere, that would be the nearest place he got fish. He just cycled around all day until he got his boxes empty and then he would go back, maybe to Port Seton I suppose. It was just an ordinary two-wheeled bicycle so it was a heavy load for him. It was quite hilly—not so bad as in this part of the country down by Saughland and those places—but he cycled.

And then down by Halltree and those places there was a man came wi' a horse and cart from Galashiels selling fish. It was usually fresh herring. You hadnae much choice, although the wee shop in the village at

Heriot kept the cured fish. So you could buy kippers and haddock and that sort o' thing, but cured. And then there was salt fish. Great big fish, cod I think it was, salted. You hung that outside the door to get rid of some of the salt then boiled it and ate it with potatoes. I never liked fish and I don't eat fish yet.

We got soup almost every day. We got kale—they call it Scotch broth now—and potato soup and lentil and rice soup. Rice was my favourite. But that was made with a piece of meat, the cheapest piece o' meat—wi' the back, the thin bit that goes over the side of the sheep or the bullock. That was much cheaper than the other meats.

We ate steam puddings, cloutie dumplings. In the winter time we had a cloutie dumpling every fortnight, or maybe just an ordinary steam pudding, a treacle pudding. We were lucky because my mother was a good cook and we were well fed.

In the houses we lived in there were generally two rooms. In Cowbraehill there was six rooms: it was the farm house we lived in there. The farmer didn't live there, my father was looking after the farm and we lived in it. But there was no bathroom in it and you had to carry the water in and any water you used you had to carry that out again. The water was coming out of a pipe in the hillside, quite near the door, and there was a trough below which was handy for lifting out water that you were goin' to use just for washing up and that sort o' thing. And then we had a water barrel to catch the rain water from the roofs, and we washed wi' that.

It was quite a chore carrying the water in. I carried the water in when I was older, after I was about ten or eleven. My brother younger than me, he and I kept the pails full. My mother would tell us to go for water and we brought it home. It stood on a bench in the pantry.

In the houses we lived in that had only two rooms, unlike Cowbraehill, they generally had an attic that you just went up a ladder to, and the boys slept up there. It was a floored attic. Then the girls were in the one room downstairs and my parents were in the other one.

I had four sisters but of course there was two of my sisters away out to work before I came along. They lived away from home. But the other three of us slept in one bed, my two sisters and me. I was very small then. And we were quite comfortable. In the attic no more than two o' the boys were in each bed. I had a bed to myself by the time that I was grown up, because my younger sister was a grocer and she lived with the grocer's people. I thought I was lucky to have a room to myself: you could bring in your chums. And we took the ribbons off our hats and put on new ones and all those sort of things. That's how we spent our time. And then of course we had to knit because the men's socks were all home-knitted.

On Friday night we all had a bath. There was a big fire put on in the room—that's the bedroom I used to occupy. The boys were all washed, bathed, and away to their beds. And then we were bathed and away to our beds. That was the Friday night regular thing, so that we were clean.

Saturday was house-cleaning day. My sister and I took part in that. My mother hadnae much time for cleaning, because she kept us all fed. And then the washings were big affairs—twice a week, Tuesdays and Fridays. All the clothes were washed and ironed and prepared for the next week. Sometimes my mother did the washing. After I grew up I did it.

In all the houses we were in when I was a girl it was much the same. You had what you called the washing pot. It was a big pot and it hung on the swee and you heated the water on that. You had the tub on a tub stool. You washed the white clothes first and then they were put on to boil, because white things had all to be boiled. Then you washed the coloured things, stockings and that sort o' thing, while they were boiling. Then that came out and you washed dusters and aprons and all the odd things that was left. So it was a big job. That was the kind of thing I was doing while I was still at school, to help mother. And if one of the neighbours was ill all the other neighbours went and tidied up the house and did the washing for them.

Neighbours helped each other. We were just like sisters and brothers to each other. I still have a friend I've had since ever she was born next door to me. I'm four years older than her. She is in London now but we have been friends right through the years. Among our neighbours there was no quarrelling or spite or anything like that. We generally had neighbours. When we were at Saughland a lot o' men worked there. There was six pair of horses so there were six ploughmen.

The work o' the ploughmen was run like an army I would say. The men had to be into the stable at six o'clock in the morning and have their horses harnessed and turned in the stall ready to come out. The grieve came in, took his watch out of his pocket and said, "Time, boys," and they all went away to their work. You had to have discipline, of course.

The ploughmen went out in order of their seniority. The first ploughman was first. And at night he was first coming back. The other ploughmen couldnae stop until

12

the first ploughman stopped. He decided when to stop by looking at his watch. The grieve told him when to go out in the morning but he didn't tell him any more until the next morning. The grieve himself didn't work at all. Maybe he would do a bit of threshing—they had a threshin' mill on the farm and if they were running short of corn for the horses he would maybe do a bit of threshing. But he didnae actually do the work. He was the grieve making sure the others did the work.

The ploughmen had a quarter of an hour at eight o'clock to take breakfast, and then they stopped at 11 a.m. and started at 1 p.m. They had a dinner break of two hours but that was for the sake of the horses. The horses were brought back, unharnessed and fed, and it was two hours before they were harnessed again. The ploughmen would go away back to the stables about half past twelve and get their horses ready to go out again. When they brought the horses in the grieve or foreman went round the stalls and fed them their oats. He didn't trust the men to do that. That was the common practice, not just my father's. You see, they had a measure of oats for each horse and they had to be sure that they got that measure and no less and no more. The ploughmen weren't trusted to do that. As soon as the men got to the stable they just took the harness off their horses and tied them up in the stall and went home for their own dinner. They had about an hour-and-a-half for their dinner. Then they went back and brushed down the horses and had a chat wi' each other. At one o'clock the grieve came in again and ordered them out.

The ploughmen used to work from one o'clock until three and they got a quarter of an hour break and then they worked until six o'clock. But that finished when I would be about sixteen, round about 1912. That was about the time the Union came in. And then they stopped at five o'clock. The Union succeeded in reducing the ploughmen's working hours by one a day. And then about that time they got the Saturday half-day. That happened as soon as the Union was set up. The Union made the rules and the farmer had to adhere to it. That was the Scottish Farm Servants' Union and it was very successful to begin with.[3]

When the ploughmen finished at six o'clock that meant they finished in the field. They still had to come in and take the harness off the horses, brush the horses down, make them comfortable, bed them up with straw for the night. And then the men would go and clean harness. They had to do that. That was the only time they got to keep their horses. They were supposed to finish at maybe half-past six, after they got the harness off and the horses bedded up. So they were working six days, Saturdays as well, from six in the morning with a quarter-hour break, two hours for dinner, part of which they spent tending to the horses, then quarter of an hour break in the afternoon and working on until six o'clock. Then they had about half-an-hour's stable work, at least half-an-hour. Then the men took turn about at being stableman on Sundays. They would have to go on Sunday morning, Sunday midday and Sunday evening to feed and water the horses and see that they were comfortable. And then washing the horses' feet in muddy weather and all those things—that was a' done in the men's time. Oh, it was a long working day they had.

I remember all that very clearly on the farms where I lived as a girl, because my brothers were ploughmen and

I knew what they were doing. They loved their horses and liked the work. They took a pride in their work and there was competition among them who could draw the straightest furrow with their horse. They were all like that, or most of them. You'd get a careless one here and there but most of them wanted to do their best, to keep your own place a wee bit further forward than the next one. They knew the ploughmen on the next farm, you see, and they werenae goin' to let their farm down for the want o' trying.

My father never joined the Union. He wouldn't pay a penny. He just thought trade unions weren't needed. He was a strong Liberal, always. He wasn't a member of the Liberal Party, but he always voted Liberal. He didn't approve of the Union but my mother did. She didn't join but my brothers were all in the Union.

How the Union began, well, it was a draper in Pathhead, Andrew Dodds, he was very strong for the Union. He got his living from the ploughmen, from the farm people, because he sold them all their clothes. He had a shop in Pathhead and then he got some o' the ploughmen. And then there was a man called Rothney, he was the real organiser. He was the General Secretary. But I remember he was killed from his bicycle: he struck a banking or something, got thrown off, and broke his neck. That was before the First World War, maybe a couple o' year before, maybe 1912. It was just when they were forming the Union.[4]

It was a chap called Wullie Drysdale that came to our farm to form the Union. He came from Cousland, above Dalkeith. He was a ploughman all his life. My sister married his brother, that's how we knew him so well. But of course we had met Wullie before that because he came round on his bicycle and got the money. They needed money to start up their Union and keep things going. Wullie wasn't active in a Union until Andrew Dodds and Rothney and those other people started. Wullie's father was a grieve and Wullie and one of his brothers worked at Cousland. He would be maybe between thirty and forty years of age when he formed the Union. He came to our house because we were friendly wi' them, my sister being married to his brother. But of course both o' his brothers was killed in the War later on.

Well, Wullie just came to our house, explaining what was happening about the Union. And of course we read it in the papers, the daily papers. And then they had a ploughmen's Union paper, just a small magazine sort o' thing. I think it was the *Scottish Farm Servants' Union Journal* it was called.[5] I knew Andrew Dodds well, of course, wi' him being the draper's shop. He'd always been a draper but he was interested in the life o' the farm people and he thought that they deserved to have a better living. He would be middle-aged about the time he took up the Union.

A lot of the farm people were Labour, but they were mostly Liberal. Wullie Drysdale was a 'Red'—Labour. I cannae just mind if he was Independent Labour Party or Labour Party. I didnae pay much attention to them, it was just hearing them all talking. My brother Jim, that's the one younger than me, he was a ploughman all his life of course so he listened to them, but I don't think I paid much attention to them really.

There was once a strike. My father didn't strike, of course. He thought they were daft. Well, that was the farmers' union didn't want to pay the money. They didn't want to listen to the Union at all. So that's what

16

the strike was about. It was the Union's advice to the men to go on strike. That was the only way they were going to get the higher wage. Quite a few ploughmen on other farms went on strike, but my brother Jim never went on strike. That was just before the 1914 War broke out. The strike lasted a very short time. The farm workers were successful. So the farmers paid up.[6]

Oh, it was a very strong Union. Some of the older ones werenae in favour of it, but the younger farm workers were.

I didn't know many of the women farm workers then because I wasnae a constant farm worker. I went out when they were busy. I never worked along wi' other girls. By the time I came along there was just myself most places where my father was because he was more or less working the farm wi' the help o' my brother and I. Around south Midlothian and north Berwickshire it wasn't very common for girls to work in the field. They would maybe start when they were fourteen and whenever they were round to maybe sixteen or seventeen they would go into service. But when my father told me to get out in the fields I went and worked! It was usually at harvest times or potato lifting and clipping, that sort o' thing. I didn't shear the sheep myself. I just rolled up the wool. And I liked that job: you had nice soft hands when you were finished.

The harvest work was, well, there was stooks in those days. You put six sheaves into a stook. You went round and round and kept them up to dry. At harvest time I worked from daylight till dark if it was dry. And I've seen us working in the moonlight to get it done. When I started first, when I was fourteen, my pay was three shillings and sixpence a week. That was working from daylight till dark, maybe sixty to seventy hours a week. But of course I wasn't out the whole week because I was in to the house to help mother wi' the churning and the different things. In 1919 the pay rose to thirty shillings a week. Before that it was sixteen shillings.

It was during the busy times that I worked—harvest and so on, and thinning turnips and any job that was really needing hurried on, I had to go out. In January ye had to carry the bags of corn. Well, first of all you had a bruiser, a sort o' grinder but we called it a bruiser, and you had to fill that wi' oats and then bruise the corn. You put that into bags and carried it and filled the corn kist. I carried the bags. I just took what I could carry, maybe about four or six stone, and you filled this big wooden kist to last the week for the horses. And then you had to put up hay into what they called the winles. You gathered up eight pound of hay or as near it as ye could and twisted it round and tucked in the ends and ye had a nice bundle. That went into a shelf behind the horses in the stable and when the men wanted to fill the hecks in the morning they just had to take a hay fork and lift them into the heck. The heck was a kind of wooden manger or rack. The horses had the hay to eat at their leisure.

And then you had to keep all the barns clean and tidy for the corn. That was a job for January, February, and March. It was an inside job. And then you had to help with the threshing when the threshing mill came in in August or September. You stood on top of the threshing mill and cut off. The sheaves were tied wi' binder twine and you stood on the top o' the mill, cut the binder twine and handed it to the man that was feeding in. You didn't fork it to him, you had to lift the sheaf, cut the string, and hand it to the man. There were two women on top of the threshing mill.

The first time I was on the mill I would just be about fifteen. It wasn't hard work. I liked it really. It was a rhythmic kind o' job. Ye widnae need to go to keep fit classes in those days!

Well, we had the threshing mill came in and threshed corn to last maybe a couple of months, or maybe three months, because they had to hire in the threshing mill. It went round the farms wi' the big steam engine and that also drove the threshing mill.

And then after the threshing of the harvest—and that went on in September, October, maybe beginning of November—you had to go and prepare the turnips, you had to shaw the turnips. That would be in late October and through November and December. It was not a very nice job but I liked it. You never felt the cold when you were shawing the turnips—you were dressed to stand the cold. We wore home-knitted mitts. Sometimes it was cold, frosty winter mornings when you were shawing, but not very often. You went to them in dry weather and got a lot into a pit so that whoever needed them would go and get them.

I never worked at potato lifting. You see, you got in a squad to lift potatoes or hired younger boys or girls, schoolchildren. They got a week—what they called the "tattie holiday"—and they came and gathered the potatoes. And they worked well. I never gathered tatties myself. I was the tea maker when the squads came in. I'd help my mother with the tea and that sort o' thing. I took the tea out to them in the field. They generally brought a pitcher themselves and some tea in it and we just poured on the water to infuse it. Then they came in at dinner time to the farm, maybe to the cart shed, and had their meal there. But in the morning and the afternoon they had the tea in the field. And maybe two o' the boys would come in then to the farm. They had two hay forks and they took an end each and the pitchers a' hanging on them and away they went.

After the turnips and potatoes I was just preparing the corn for the horses. And then the grain was all to clean. We had what we called 'fanners', that was a big wooden box sort o' thing with fanners inside and then you poured in the corn and turned a handle and cleaned – took the light corn from the good corn. The good corn was for sale and the light corn went to feed the hens and horses.

And then in July—July's the hay month—I helped to turn the hay, although they had a hay machine, a tedder, for turning over the hay. And then you put it into what we called kyles—small stacks. You did that with a hay fork and then you raked up any hay that was lying around and then you put it into what ye called ricks, and then they had big bogies that came and drove the ricks into the stacks. A kyle was just a small amount o' hay and that stood until it dried off a bit and then it went into a rick, a big stack. And then you had to make the ropes to tie the kyles down. You had a thing tied on your waist and it had a handle, there was a sort o' hook attached to a rope and a bar sort o' thing. And you stood like this all day long on a wet day making hay ropes and straw ropes. That was an inside job, in the barn.

In the summer when we were making the meadow hay my father and one o' my brothers cut it with a scythe. You couldnae get a machine in to the meadows and they cut the hay wi' a scythe. And then we raked it together and put it into ricks. And then we had to make our ropes – that was done outside. We made the ropes just where we were making the hay.

Singling turnips that was in May and June. Ye hoed the turnips and things until it was time for the hay making. Well, I've seen me doing a wee bit o' singling but no' often. I don't think that was interesting work really but I liked the turnip singling. There was usually maybe another couple of girls. The men did some but it was the girls that did quite a lot o' that.

That was the main jobs for women. And for that, well, at one time it was ten shillings a week, when I was about fifteen—that would be about 1910, 1911, 1912. And then it went up to sixteen shillings about 1912. And then it went up to thirty shillings in 1919 and after that I got married and didnae need any wages!

The Bondage Act was out and the women bondagers were out before I came along.[7] But I remember meeting older women who had been bondagers. They were living at Crichton Dean, near Pathhead. One o' them—Teenie – had been in service, and then Maggie worked at Saughland, a very big farm between Tynehead and Blackshiels. Maggie had been a bondager there all her working life. You see, that was her way to get a house. Her father was a dyker and went out building dykes all round the farm. Maggie Leitch and Jessie Whyte was bondagers and had been all their lives. They worked in Midlothian. That would be just before the 1914 War. Maggie was retired maybe a year—it would be maybe 1911. Up till then she was working as a bondager on Saughland farm.

There was usually one bondager employed for each

pair of horses—but that was before my time. Maggie Leitch was the only one I remember dressed as a bondager. She had on what we called a drugget petticoat. They were just like a type o' tartan—nicely made. Drugget's very like what the jeans are made of now, sort of denim stuff but its name was drugget. When you went to Andrew Dodds for a yard and a half of drugget he knew what you meant. They were nicely made and there was black braid round the bottom and then a row of black braid for fancy further up. They were very, very neat. And then you had a print blouse and a costume jacket, maybe a jacket that was finished for going to church. They were worn to go to church first—then they were all on their second lap for the field workers.

They had straw hats, the real bondagers had straw hats. Maggie Leitch had a straw hat, so had Jessie Whyte. It was just like a basket on their head. It was all lined wi' print, the same colour as the blouse. Aye, they were big heavy things, they were. I never had one but I had an ugly for the summer time. An ugly was just like a wee cape round your neck and then the cloth was brought over and you had to make tucks in and put canes through. It was like a beehive and kept the sun off you. That was the object of it, to keep the sun off you and keep your skin white. But the bondagers didnae wear their straw hats in the summer, they wore them in the winter. So it could have been they wore them then to keep their heads warm.

The bondagers wore home-knitted five-ply woollen stockings, and laced boots with high cuffs—there were no wellingtons in those days. So that was the sort of dress that Maggie Leitch wore. She was a woman in her sixties or seventies when I knew her—I was just a lassie. She seemed quite happy as a bondager. Neither she nor her sister were married.

There weren't squads of seasonal workers working on the farms where I lived in Midlothian. It was just the ploughmen's wives and the boys from the school. The Heriot farms didnae grow big crops of potatoes, so they just got out their ploughmen's wives and daughters, or boys if they had them, or two or three boys from the school. It was only after I got married and went to live for a time in East Lothian that I encountered seasonal workers—the tattie squads. The women, the miners' wives, generally came from Prestonpans.

Of course in Midlothian we always had the Irishmen came for the harvest. There would be maybe four to the farm we were on, each farm would employ maybe four or five—small numbers, just to help out with the harvest. They were paid the same wages as the ordinary farm workers, worked the same hours, and lived in the bothy. The bothy was like a house but with no water or sanitation in it. But mother saw to it that the Irishmen had good comfortable beds, and all their blankets were always washed and cleaned for them coming. Where we lived mother always took over and saw to them. I don't think she ever did get paid for doing that. She just did it to make the men comfortable.

Mostly the Irishmen just lived on tea and they bought their bread. But on Saturday night they brought a piece of meat each and mother made soup for them and cooked their meat and boiled a big pot o' potatoes.

There were no Irish women with them. There were Irish women came to East Lothian but none in Midlothian, just Irish men and they were always the same family. They came when my father was at just north of Brothershiels, Heriot. Well, I was very small when Jimmy Boyle started comin' because I can remember he had a concertina and he played to us. He put down a tin and my two brothers and I—just small children—danced on this tin and he learned us to dance. Oh, it was a great big sheet of tin my father must have had for something. And we used to go into the bothy beside Jimmy and his sons.

To me in those days Jimmy Boyle looked old but he would be a man about thirty or so. He had two sons with him, very young boys, just starting work. Jimmy and his boys came from Donegal. He came every year for, oh, years and years. It sort o' stopped at the First World War: he couldn't get over. And then we had to just get whoever we could. But from maybe about 1900 to 1914 the Boyles came every year.

They came in time for the harvest. Well, Jimmy would come for the singling but then we didnae need him because we didnae have a big lot o' turnips. But he would go to East Lothian where there was large crops. He would work there but he always came back to my father after for harvest time. Jimmy Boyle had done this kind of thing all his life. That was how Irish people had to get their living. There was no work for them in Ireland. They had small crofts where they were and had some hens and that sort o' thing.

The Boyles were all Catholics. I never knew of any sort o' tension between the Irish seasonal workers and the Scottish farm workers in Midlothian, never any ill feeling, never that I knew of. I can't remember the Boyles discussing politics but of course I was too small at that time—I wasnae interested, that was the trouble!

If the Boyles came for milk or anything they came into our house. But they were never in the house sitting down. They were never sort of friends in that sense, oh, no. They lived in the bothy. My brothers and I learned to dance in the bothy but that's when we were small children. We didn't go when we were older. I just don't know why that was. We just didnae mix wi' them when we got older. You know, we thought Catholics were terrible things! There was a Catholic school at Pathhead. We went to Pathhead school, a different school. We never mixed wi' a Catholic then. Oh, there was very, very strong feeling. I cannae say I can remember any fights between Catholic children and non-Catholics. But we just had that feeling that there was something wrong wi' them! Which was a shame, because their religion was all the difference, you see.

Jimmy Boyle and his sons didnae join the Scottish Farm Servants' Union. Oh, no, they were masters' men, oh, very much so. It showed in the way they worked when they saw the boss coming, that sort of thing. They worked harder then, although they were good workers. They seemed to think that the master was somebody worth bowing tae! They were afraid of losing their jobs, that's what it was, I think. And they were afraid of joining the Union because o' the same reason, I'm sure. I suppose they could have joined the Union if they wanted. But of course the younger ones were rough living—wild Saturday nights.

Well, they all met off all the different farms, the Irishmen. And then when they got drunk they started to fight among themselves. They met in Stow. They would have to walk there or go by train. You could go by train from Heriot to Stow. But I don't suppose they would go by train, I think they would just walk. It would be about three-and-a-half to four miles. Well, there were fights just among the Irish but it was all forgotten on the Sunday morning and they would all be away to chapel!

The nearest chapel was Pathhead. That was the only chapel that I knew of, the only one in south Midlothian.[8]

Each of my brothers—and I had six brothers—began as a ploughman. They had to stay at home for maybe a couple of years or so. Then they left the farm whenever they could. Only two of them liked the farm: Adam, my third brother, he was much older than me, and then Jim, the fourth brother, the one that was at Edgehead, they liked the farm. But the others just wanted away to other jobs. Of course the Saturday afternoon work took a lot of them away because they got the Saturday off in other jobs, you see. It would be about 1910 or 1911 when farm workers got the half-day off on a Saturday. Before that they worked all day on a Saturday, just like Monday to Friday. The half-day came just when the Union was forming.

Well, my eldest brother Sandy went on to the railway. He got a job at Heriot for a while and then he wanted to get more money and he went into the marshalling yard at Millerhill and worked there. Later on there was a scheme where you could get to Canada or America. You had to work on the railways for two years there. So Sandy went away on that scheme and he was in America all the rest of his life. He just worked on the railways for two years and then he got the job to be caretaker at the university at Syracuse in New York State. I've the name of the university on a plate that his wife brought me. He met her when he was at Millerhill. She was a dressmaker.

Well, she went out there and she was linen maid at the university and he was caretaker. My fifth brother, Dave, was a wanderer: he was wherever there was big money going! He wandered about. He was in Canada for about three weeks and came home—he didnae like it. But he was away to wherever there was good money, like draining and dyking and fencing. But he got a job in the woods at Selkirk and he met a girl, got married and settled down there. Then he worked for the Council after that in Selkirk.

Jim, my fourth brother, he was on the farm most o' his life. He was in the wood-cutting contracts for a while and then he got married and of course the only way to get a house was to take a job on the farm. But I think he liked farming fine. He was a quiet chap. So he stayed on the farm.

John, the youngest one of the six, he was thirteen years younger than me, he left home when he was sixteen and went into Edinburgh to work wi' St Cuthbert's Co-operative. He was a driver. He was killed in a road accident a few years ago. He wasn't quite retiring age at that time.

Two of my brothers went off to fight in the 1914–18 War. The American brother Sandy, him that was in America, he came over with the American army. And then Wullie, my second eldest brother, he was working wi' a wood contractor but he joined up. And he got shot, wounded through the arm. They were sleeping in a hay stack and there were Germans on the other side of the hay stack. They spoke to each other and the Germans said, "Och, away you go," and whenever they went away they shot him. They killed one man and my brother was shot through the fat bit of his arm. In the next bed to him when he came home to the hospital in England was my brother Sandy from America: he had just picked up a bug of some kind. But they both survived the War.

I remember very well the 1914 War breaking out. And all the young chaps—although they could have stayed on because the army didn't take farm folk—oh, they were getting handed white feathers and a' this sort of thing at Fountainhall and Heriot. It was the young ladies, farmers' daughters, they were going round handing them white feathers.

They were just young chaps, about seventeen or eighteen years old. They hadn't volunteered but there were none of them really of age to go. However, eighteen of them then all banded together from the farms round Fountainhall and went into Edinburgh and joined up. None of them came back. None. Well, there was one man came back but he was an Irishman that had come to work casual. But none of those young chaps came back. They were all killed.

Oh, it was terrible, dreadful. It was them all, it was the youth of the district. They'd all gone in a body to volunteer. I think they just felt it was going to be fun. Well, you see, we was all led to believe that the War would be over in two months. Well, war broke out on August 4th and they were all away before Christmas. And none of them came back.

Most of them was in the K.O.S.B. but one or two was in the Highland Light Infantry.[9] I knew them all. I worked beside them, you see. They were all working on the farms around the village and they had gone to the Fountainhall school and been brought up in the district. But that's what happened. The effect on Fountainhall of the deaths of these young fellows, oh, ye couldnae describe it. Some of the mothers never got over it.

I mentioned Fountainhall school. Well, when we were at Halltree as children we went a while to Heriot school and then we went to the other places. We went to Pathhead school, or Crichton school they called it. It's just at the top of the village in Pathhead. And we had a long road to walk there. It would be about five miles a day we walked—two-and-a-half miles there and two-and-a-half miles back. I was ten when we went to Pathhead school. But I started school when I was six. I had a very long way to go then but my second oldest brother Wullie used to carry me part of the way! Oh, there were no school buses in those days.

I liked the school, yes, I did, I liked the school.

When father moved from job to job the farmer you were going to sent the horses and carts to lift your stuff. It was quite a common sight to see farm workers flitting in those days on the 28th of May. That was the end of the year and the term date at Whitsun. That other one was the November term. We called it Martinmas dowie.

I remember the feeing marts or labour markets where the farm workers were hired. Dalkeith was the 14th of March and men that wanted a job had to go to Dalkeith. We called it the fair, Dalkeith fair.[10] The men just stood about the street and the farmer went and talked to them. It was just once a year and the men just was standing aboot the street. They didn't wear any special clothing or a button in their lapel or anything like that. The farmers just went and spoke to them. It was always the farmer that spoke to the men, not the men to the farmer.

I never went to the hiring fair myself. And my father

was never hired at a fair. He always had a job before he went to another one. But I remember being in Dalkeith when these hiring fairs were on. We went to Dalkeith and we went to the Corn Exchange and had penny reels. The man that wanted ye to dance wi' him paid a penny to the hall. That was the 14th of March— a very big occasion. Well, you see, farm workers and working people didnae get out as they do now, no. So once a year there was this big social occasion. The young men and young women were all in, and if they wanted to dance wi' ye they had to pay a penny towards the hall, or towards a fiddler or something. Och, it was a good social day.

I think I would be about seventeen the first time I was at the penny reel in the Corn Exchange. My older sister accompanied me. I don't think my parents minded even if I went myself to the penny reel. But things were different then. People had more respect for the women folk of the district. It was just before the First War that I used to go to the penny reels at Dalkeith. There were buses running between Blackshiels and Dalkeith.

Usually the hiring at the fair was all done before midday. The farmers didnae stay after that. And the men all got hired up to new places. Some people went to a new place every year. If they were hired on the 14th of March they had to work on the farm where they were until the end of the May term.

And then of course on the night before the fair the farmer saw all the men and asked them if they would stay on, or if they were stayin' or if they were leavin'. And if they could make a bargain wi' the farmer they stayed on. But the farmer asked the men, it wasnae the men asked the farmer. If the farmer didn't ask a man if he were stayin' on then the man knew he had to go. The farmer didnae speak to a man at all if he didnae want him to stay. That was more or less the push! He was gettin' the heave. I don't remember anything like that happening on any farm I was living on.

The farm workers and their wives didn't seem to worry about being on the move so often as some of them were. It was just a way of life, you see. And they liked a new place every year. I had an uncle and they moved every year. "Och," he says, "they take ye for granted if ye bide too long wi' them. A year's fine." And then he'd move in Midlothian or to Berwickshire, or wherever he could get a place that he fancied. That was before the First War.

He was married, that uncle, and they had two girls and two boys. Their schooling must have suffered wi' all those moves from one farm to another. They would be in a different school every year. But then they grew up to be farm workers, you see. Education wasn't so important, it didn't mean anything to them, not then. However, they all did quite well when they grew up. It was just a way of life, you see, they just liked to get in the carts and move on.

I heard a story—it might just be a story. An old farmer said to the man, "Now just bide on, Geordie." "Oh," he says, "I'd like to bide on but ye ken the wife." "Well," says the farmer, "I'll tell ye what tae dae. Take a cairt and gie her a hurl on the term day. But," he says, "bide on."

They didnae have much to pack in those days. They didnae have the things we have now—there were nae food mixers! Furniture, well, they had one easy chair for the man of the house always, and just maybe a table and small chairs, and the beds of course. And of course there was no mattresses in those days. We slept on chaff, big bags filled with chaff, what we called tikes. They were clean because you had fresh tikes twice a year, oh, very comfortable and very warm. We'd always good blankets, blankets were plentiful.

There werenae wardrobes in those days. There would be in other houses but not in the small houses we lived in. You had a chest of drawers for keepin' the Sunday clothes in. And of course in the kitchen ye had what you'd call a display cabinet now: the best china was in the top and the food and stuff down below. And then you had a kist, or maybe two or three, to hold your wearing clothes. You never put on your Sunday clothes through the week. So they werenae big flittings when they took place. Two carts held the lot—and the family! There were no washing machines or spin dryers, televisions or radios in those days.

How the folk passed their time, well, the men cleaned the horses' harness and sat in the stable and sung. You've heard o' corn kisters, well, that's what the corn kisters were—men singing without any music.[11] It was mostly mouth music and sometimes some fiddle music. An odd person would have a melodeon or something like that.

In our house there were books o' all kinds. So there was much reading done. You generally had to lend each other books and buy some. There was nothing like a public library then. And then you got all the weekly papers. We got the *Weekly Scotsman* and the *Weekly News*, and there was different sort o' papers. We always got the *Daily Record* and the *Edinburgh Evening News*. Somebody went to the station for the *Evening News*. But we weren't allowed to read Sunday papers, oh, no!

When I was a girl my mother would go away maybe once a month to Gorebridge or Stow or some o' them places. And then we'd get a bundle of comics and that sort o' thing, once a month. And then you'd read them and pass them on to other children that had none. And then we got the *People's Friend* and *The Welcome* and magazines o' one kind an' another.[12]

The parish minister visited homes regularly. We had a great respect for the minister. I remember when I was at Borthwick school—that's when we were at Cowbraehill – I got out at three o'clock and my brothers and sister didn't get out until four. So I was always wandering about in Borthwick waiting for them, and I mind old Mr Wardlaw the minister, he used to give me two and sometimes four sweeties, English Mixtures, sugary things. And, mind you, I was bound to be hungry but I didn't eat those sweeties. I carried them home and my mother divided them up among the smaller ones in our family. But I still remember those sweeties, white ones and pink ones. Oh, I was sorely tempted to eat them myself, but then I got them from the minister.[13]

The biggest disappointment ever I got in my life was when I was invited to the manse Christmas party and Sunday School party. You see, the minister said to my mother, "Oh, those children can't come to the Sunday School. I couldn't expect them to come when they're walking all that way to the village school five days a week. But," he says, "I'll give you some cards and you teach them and then I'll see them from time to time." So Christmas came round and we were invited to the manse Christmas party and Sunday School party at Borthwick.

My father got us all into a cart, horse and cart, and went by Tynehead and picked up the children there. When we got to the manse the tea was in the kitchen. And it was just scones and pancakes. I don't know what I had been expecting but I got an awful drop. That's just what we got at home every Sunday! It was nothing special. But I've never forgotten that.

Now I met my husband in 1914, when I was nineteen. Well, war broke out that year. We had to make whist drives and dances to make money to get money for soldiers' parcels and socks and balaclavas, and we knitted all those. So that's how we got money. Everybody gave scones, pancakes and stuff free, and we got the money for buying wool and that sort o' thing. Well, that's where I met him. He was a farm worker at that time. He worked a wee bit away at first and then he moved quite near us. He was a ploughman. And then him and two o' his pals took a wood-cutting contract and he was on that for about three years before we were married. He wasn't taken away to the war, though he was on call. Him and my brother they were both waiting for their call-up when the armistice was signed. Oh, we all were very relieved at that. So we were married just at the end of 1918, just as the war ended. Well, he worked on that wood contract and then we moved into Edinburgh and he worked wi' Smart, a haulage contractor. And then we moved back to Corsehope again, back to the country, and he built dykes and did fencing and a' that sort o' thing. Oh, he never worked as a ploughman again—he didn't like the job. He just hated it. He used to always say, "Oh, my God, go to that end, turn and come back." He meant the horses and plough, you know. Well, my husband died in 1967. We had just the one daughter, Nancy. I'd always been a tenant before, but when my husband died I bought this house where I'm living now at Loanhead. It gives me a sense of independence.

Mrs Belle Lindsay

I was born in September 1895 at a farm they called The Murrays, quite near Pathhead. My father was farm grieve at that place. He was born at Cousland round about 1858 or 1859. He was seventy-eight when he died and that was in 1936.

My father's father was a blacksmith at Cousland. But I don't know anything about my great-grandfather.

My mother's maiden name was Denholm and she was born up the hills there at Maudslie. And then they went down to Stagebank at Heriot and from there to Lanarkshire, and all the rest of the family was born there—six sons and four daughters. My mother was the second oldest. She died in 1950 and she was eighty-six the day after her funeral, so she must have been born in 1864, maybe five or six years younger than my father.

My mother's family were all on the farm when they were young and they gradually drifted off to the railways and nearly all went foreign. In fact, they all went foreign except one uncle and he died at Grantshouse. The others all went abroad—two went to Canada, one went to Australia, one to New Zealand. One o' my uncles went to working on the railway in South Africa and then he went to the gold mines there. Well, there wouldnae be enough work on the farm for them at home and there werenae much money goin' for it either. Oh, it was

35

quite common for people to go abroad to work when I was young. It never entered my heid, no, never, that I should go abroad myself. But I still keep up wi' some o' my cousins abroad.

I think my father and mother was married about five years afore I came along. We hadnae much o' a family. There was just the three of us. Well, there wur five year and a half between me and my sister and there wur just two years between my sister and my brother. I'm the oldest.

Well, we went from The Murrays to Hilltown near Edmonstone, and we went from there to Corsehope out at Heriot. I would just be about two when we went to Corsehope. And I mind the Boer War was on while we were there and they couldnae get workers and my mother went to the harvest. Well, a lot of men went to the war and there was nobody to help them out wi' the harvest. I just couldnae put my hands on it the now but I've a box that Queen Victoria gave to the soldiers during the Boer War. My uncle that went to South Africa sent one home. I really couldnae say why so many farm workers went off to fight in the Boer War. I was young. I didnae ken much aboot it.

When my father and mother got married about 1890 his wages were sixteen shillings a week. That was his wage and it was paid once in six month. The hours of work were six in the morning tae six at night, seven days a week. They'd to go out to do the horses on the Sunday. Of course there was no Saturday half-days then.

My father had been quite young when he became a grieve. Well, when they were new married they took up house at Nettingflat out at Heriot. My mother often told me they got their wages once in six month. And the farmer brought the flour to bake and oatmeal, and meal for the pig—they had a pig. And they had to go out at the time when the potatoes was lifted and gathered them. They gathered the big ones for domestic use and the wee ones to feed the pigs. And when they wanted coal they came into Arniston Pit lies and maybe three or four had carts a' at once, maybe more than that, and they a' got half a ton o' coal. And that a' came off the wages at the end of the six months. That was afore I came along. So I suppose it was at the term time father was paid, Whitsun and the November term likely.

So as I say when I was two we went to live at Corsehope at Heriot. My father wasnae the grieve there. He was driving horses at Corsehope: he had been a grieve and then he went back to being a ploughman. He was in the Farm Servants' Union. I dinnae mind much aboot it but I always remember he had a badge wi' a man ploughin' with a pair o' horses. He always wore it.

He was quite active in the Union. I think him and someone out o'er the country there sort o' started it. That was when he was at Carrington Barns. But he never made nae fuss about the Union. He just went to the meetings, as far as I mind anyway. I was young then and I wasnae really interested.

After the First World War my father left the land and went to work in the pit—the Gore pit up at Arniston. That was the only pit he worked in, as long as I mind onyway. When we came to Carrington there were a lot o' pit workers went from here. They lived in Carrington but went to work in the Gore pit and the Emily at Gorebridge. And there used to be a pit they ca'ed the Vogrie—some o' them went to that. And then some went to the Lady Victoria tae at Newtongrange.

It was after oo'd been at Carrington Barns farm for five years my father decided he'd go to the pit. I think it was the money. They had poor wages on the farm then. I cannae mind latterly what he got but as I say when they were married it was sixteen shillings a week. So he was in the pits up till he retired and then he went back just taking jobs at his own hand. Just before he died he was working at Stonefield Hill, that's a farm just near Rosewell. I remember him being tired. He was feeding the mill and he came out and I remember him hanging on to the door gasping for breath. That was on the Friday night. And I got the doctor and it was pneumonia he had. He was awfy ill on the Monday morning and I phoned for the doctor again. The doctor came and gave him an injection and said he would be back at twelve o'clock. My father was dead before the doctor went to Gorebridge. It was as quick as that.

The houses we lived in that I remember were very poor. Well, the water was to carry in and carry out: no inside water, no sanitation, no toilet. It was up the garden. The houses had cement floors. We just had linoleum in the room and a bit carpet in front o' the bed. Some were two-roomed houses, some o' them was just the one room. The house that I do remember best was when oo was at Corsehope, when I was wee. We lived away up on the hill, and quite comfortable, you know. But the house was just a room and kitchen and a wee back kitchen place—they ca'ed it the pantry in thae days.

When I started at the school my father was on a farm at Hermiston, the other side o' Edinburgh. Well, I started at Hermiston school. Oo was just a year there—the ploughmen flitted about every year then, went away for the least thing!—and we went to a place they called Broomhouse. Oo was there two year and then oo came tae Upper Dalhousie, down the road there frae Carrington. And oo was two year there and then oo came to Carrington Barns. A' thae flittings affected my schooling, oh, it did, it did. Well, when I started at Hermiston school I went along yon road, one and a half miles, and over the canal bridge.[14] It was just the done thing and nobody went but myself. And then when we went down to Broomhouse I went to Corstorphine school, which was a big school. Of course we were just there a year when away oo went again and oo came to Dalhousie and I went to Cockpen school for a wee while. And then when oo came to the Barns at Carrington here I was twelve and a half and I was at Carrington school until I was fourteen.

I did not like the school. Well, you see I have a swollen jaw? That was an accident at the school. And I took lock-jaw and the doctor came to me and forced my mouth open and pulled my teeth and he broke my jaw bone. So I was taken away to the Sick Children's Hospital. But my jaw had never been properly set and there was just something grew up where the bone should have been. I had to go back and get that taken out, but I was always growing, wi' the result it deformed my face. And I've often thought my father and mother was very simple to let that pass, though of course they wouldnae have money to fight it.

So I didnae like the school very much, until I got older. I just don't know why I didnae like it—maybe I was too stupid! I likit singing and sewing, that sort o' thing. But when I came to Carrington school we'd an awfy hard taskmaster, the school master. Brunton was his name. He lived in the school house. Oh, he was very severe. He gave me the strap and I've seen him put the boys over his knee and giein' them it on the behind and a', for very little.

There wur a junior teacher took the wee ones and she learnt ye—there was no sewing mistress came in yon days—how to sew and knit.

When I left school I just went to the farm. I got six shillings a week. That was for working from six in the morning till six at night, same as my father. Everybody did the same. I worked all day on a Saturday but, oh, no' Sunday. It was a six-day week, twelve hours a day, seventy-two hours a week, for six shillings. It was a poor wage. I often felt I could have run away.

When I was just eighteen I came to Carrington Mains to work. There was an empty house and ye used to get it if ye worked for it—a free house, see. And I was just to do this for a year but it went on for five year, ten year. The farmer, they called him Inch. His son managed the farm from Lempock Wells away at Pencaitland. He came every week wi' wages and organised things, you see. And, oh, they were far, far behind wi' their work. Well, we came to Carrington in the month o' May and my mother was papering the house. It had been standing empty and was a' needing done up. So I was having to have two or three days to help her and they came round – it was a Wednesday—and said would I start on the Thursday morning.

The first job I got—sowing turnips. Somebody said, "Are you frightened for horses?" I said, "No, I'm no' frightened for horses." I was fond o' horses, I'd grown up wi' them wi' my father being a ploughman and I'd often spent time in the stables wi' them. So that was my first job, sowing turnips.

You just walked up and down, up and down and filled the machine wi' the seed. There was no problem wi' the horse. Then the other jobs I did, I led in, in the harvest time. The harvest was a lot o' hard work. Of course there was no combines. And if it was good weather they worked on a Sunday. Oh, it was hard work forking yon big sheaves up! It was a two-horse binder but I never drove the binder, I was aye stookin'. By the end o' the harvest ye was exhausted, I'd say that.

And I rolled wi' the horse, and hay making. I never shawed turnips, I singled them. Oh, that job—it wasnae peyed for what ye did! It was three halfpence for 100 yards. Ye'll ken we singled a guid bit for that. Oh, it was an awfy dreary job that, terrible, terrible. But I never shawed turnips because it was just to feed the cattle in the winter time so I never was oot.

The time o' the War—the First War—I did ploughing. I was just a big lassie then, I wouldnae be ony mair than nineteen when the war broke out. The men on the farm, well, they were a' past gaun to the war, they were too old. I never came in contact wi' any o' the younger men that went off to the war. I didnae know any personally.[15]

When I came to work at Carrington Mains just before the War I got ten shillings a week and a free house. I would just be coming up for nineteen. They put value on the house, you see. A free house—they were goin' tae put value on that, and the house wisnae valued at very much, I don't mind tellin' ye. Well, you see, the house was there and my father went to the pit and I was just to do it for a year but it just went on—ten year I was round at the farm at Carrington Mains.

I was what they ca'ed a bondager. Well, ye had a sort o'—they ca'ed them uglies. I mind I made my own. It was a print material, then you got bone and you put it round the front. It was to keep the sun off ye. Noo everybody wants the sun! But they had straw hats an' a' though. But I made my ugly myself. I was kind o' guid-handed then. I wore it just the summer. In the winter I wore a tammy, I think. All the women on the farm wore these uglies. They were a' what they ca'ed bondagers.

There would be a lot o' women like that in Midlothian then. A lot o' my friends were bondagers. And then some o' them drifted away to service. That was your only alternative. I thought on goin' but then it was this tied to the house, ye see. I aye felt it was my duty to stick to the house. I looked after my parents till they died. I was the eldest of the family.

If it hadn't been for that I had every intention o' goin' to domestic service. Well, the conditions in domestic service werenae much better as the fields. You maybe got your meat but you didnae have big wages. But some o' my friends went to Edinburgh to work in domestic service, the most of them went to the town. And my sister went to service. She was the maid at Carrington Mains farm there for years. That was the choice—the farm or domestic service, there was nothing else. There was no office work, carpet factory or paper mill. None of the girls went to factories till during the First War.

You had to be ready to go to the field at six o'clock. So ye had to be up about quarter past five maybe. Ye had a bit tea and bread then, but no porridge—you had porridge at night. I suppose the men did the stables for me. I had my own pair o' horse belonging to the farm. But the men cleaned them and looked after them for me. They didn't expect me to do it. But I took my horses out to the field every morning. Oh, aye, I was never frightened for horses.

So ye started at six o'clock and worked I think till twelve. You took a piece wi' ye and a flask o' tea. That was supposed to be your breakfast, about nine o'clock. The tea was cold by this time. Oh, I had many cold, cold days in the fields!

We wore heavy clothes. They were made o' the material they ca'ed drugget. It was sort o' waterproof material—coarse, awfy coarse and, oh, it was heavy. And there werenae wellingtons in yon days, mind. I wore big heavy boots, well, they were just as heavy as men's.

You would just take your tea and piece about nine, then start again. And then you got an hour for your dinner, twelve till one, then started again and went on until six at night. You wasnae supposed to get a break in the afternoon but maist of folk did have one. It was the same again—tea and bread! And then you stopped at six but you wouldnae get home till half past six easy. It was a long day.

We had a good meal in the middle o' the day, soup, potatoes and pudding—long syne everybody made dumplings, cloutie dumplings, apple pie and apple dumpling. The meat was, well, just mutton or steak. Steak wasnae dear in thae days. But everybody ate mutton. I never was very fond o' it—greasy—but plenty of folk ate mutton. And of course they had the garden so ye'd aye plenty vegetables. There used to be plenty carts come round wi' fruit. Of course, when oo were movin' round frae farm to farm we missed vegetables and fruit—apart from here at Carrington. There used to be two or three vans came here. And then when we was down at Broomhouse we was just, oh, ten minutes from the shops at Corstorphine. That was handy. And the like o' Dalhousie, there used to be vans come there.

At tea time, after six o'clock, we would get a cooked meal, maybe ham and eggs or fish or something. There were plenty eggs and plenty milk. But we didnae make our own cheese, no, no, none round about here. You had to pay for the milk of course ye got from the farm. Then long syne my mother had a pig till we came to this side. All the farm workers used to have pigs. I think if it had been now I couldnae have eaten a pig efter I had fed it!

I remember the hiring fair at Dalkeith, oh, that used to be a great time. It was in February. I never went to the hiring myself but I went to the shows on the Saturday! At the hiring fair they went down and they seemed tae ken whether the farmers were looking for men or no' and then I suppose they went up and settled up what they were goin' to get and a' the rest o' it. And then they got what they ca'ed the arles. The arles were about ten shillings or something. It was an agreement, sort o'.[16]

Plenty women went to the hiring fair, though mind there was no transport from here at Carrington then. If ye was goin' to Dalkeith ye had to walk. It will be aboot five mile easy. It's a good bit to walk but you never thought nothing about it.

The hiring fair was just the open street, away down

the High Street, at the Corn Exchange. Well, on the fair day they had dancing in the Corn Exchange.

The fair was every February and then it was transferred to March. It was after the First War the change was made, if I remember right. Then the hiring fair went on for two or three years after the war, but no' very long. And then the farm workers gradually drifted off the farm. Carrington Mains was a big farm. Elderly people that's away now's told me that they remember when they had twelve outside workers round there and seven pair o' horses. Now there's just the farmer and his son and one man.

I cannae say I remember the very earliest o' the First World War. Well, the lads that I kent that went they aye kept to write, and I kept knitting socks and sending this, that and something else, ye ken. The like o' my brother-in-law was away and his brother, thae laddies was a' away. My brother-in-law went to the navy. They belonged the village. My brother was ower young to go. There were many laddies frae Carrington killed in the War. I know a lot o' them. Aye, it was a sad time.

My husband had been at the War. He was on the farm early on and then just before the War he went to the Gore pit, Arniston. And of course when the War came he joined up. He was away four year in France and Gaza. They let the miners away early, ye ken, demobbed them early. He started back in the pit again. He was best man at the wedding o' a man that worked in the pit wi' him. I was best maid. That's how I met him. We got married in 1923. I was twenty-seven then. Oh, it was a relief all right when I no longer had to work in the fields! I ken I looked forward to gettin' married right enough.

When I got married I got a house. It's no' there now.

45

It's been added on to another one down the village. It had a living room, one wee bedroom and a wee kitchenette thing. There was no water inside. Ye had to carry the water in and out an' a'. So our house when we got married had a toilet up the garden—a dry closet. The pail had to be emptied—oh, a terrible job that! And that went on for years. We was seven years doon there. Then we came up to that house at the corner, goin' up the Temple road. It's two into one now. We was in there eleven years.

When we came to Carrington there was one pump in the middle o' the village. That was just before the First War. At that time I dinnae think there would be as many as a hundred folk in Carrington. Of course there was big families, mind. There were families down the village, three o' them anyway, had nine of a family.

My husband was in the pit until he retired. But he had a very bad accident in the pit: got both his legs broken at once. He never worked for two years, so he never was down again efter that. He worked on the pithead efter that, always the Gore up at Arniston.

When we came to Carrington just before the 1914 War there were a lot o' pit workers went from Carrington. My husband went to the pit on his bicycle. Oh, they had to start early in the mornin'. So he got up aboot five and went away aboot six. They started lettin' them doon about half past six—well, it micht hae been six o'clock, I cannae mind. But it was an early rise and early to bed! I would make up his piece, he had a tin box and I just made sandwiches. Tea was cold, of course. Some o' them just took water, but my husband Dave always took tea. But ye couldnae keep it hot. There was nae thermos, it was just a tin bottle.

Oh, that was a different life from what I was used tae before I got married. When I got married I gave up working in the fields. My mother was beginning to get sort of frail—I went and helped her. Oh, I preferred bein' a housewife to workin' in the fields, oh, much more so! I never wanted to go back again. Well, during the 1926 strike my brother and my husband went to the singling and then they went to hay and then they went to harvest. And there was a cottage at Middleton Mains, so oo went up, just took the bare necessities. Oh, it was hard times, the 1926 strike! It went on from June to December. I mind when my money was a' done an' a'. We had nae money coming in at a', just what they were gettin' workin' on the farm at Middleton Mains, which wasnae much. That was all my husband got while he was on strike. But he never thought o' goin' back to work permanently on the farm.

In thae days when I worked on the farms there was no such a known thing as a holiday. Maybe if the Queen was comin' tae Edinburgh you'd get a day, or something like that, but, oh, no holidays. At Christmas and New Year ye got one day, one day. There were nae summer holidays, not even a single day. There was nae May Days or onything. We had only two days off in the year— Christmas Day and New Year's Day, nothing else. We worked six days a week, seventy-two hours a week. It was a hard life!

We went to the pictures and there used to be a thing, it was a sort o' travelling theatre, a kind of side show affair come to Gorebridge. They used to put on weird things, *The Red Barn Mystery*, and *Burke and Hare* and all the creepy things! They had a picture hoose at Gorebridge and at Newtongrange. You'd still to walk if you wanted to go. There was no bus service till Cockburn started at Eskbank after the First War. I cycled all over the place. It was the only way you could get.

There were nae dancing round about except after the harvest. They had what they ca'ed a kirn. That's the only dancin' that was, once the harvest was in. The maist o' the farms had a kirn—if they had suitable accommodation. Some o' the farm workers got it up theirsel'. The farmer didnae gie any help. There's never been a kirn round at Carrington Mains or Carrington Barns, they were a' up the country. But apart from that there was nothing in my young day. It was just an existence. Ye had nae time tae yoursel', nane at a'.

I read a lot right enough and in those days it was the *People's Friend* you got. My father always got the daily paper, the *Daily Record*. It used to come frae Gorebridge wi' the postman every morning. My mother had the *Weekly Journal* and the *People's Friend*.[17] There was no library. If ye wanted books ye had to buy them. You didnae buy many and when you did buy they were cheap ones. I wasnae a great reader o' books. But my husband was, oh, he was a great reader. Well, the library van came then, you see. That was long after we were married of course. When he was in Bonnyrigg after he came back from the First War there was a library in Bonnyrigg, down Lothian Street.

Mrs Jessie Landells

We were ca'ed Hoggie's Angels. I still get that to the present day: "Jessie, you used to be a Hoggie's Angel." I says, "I ken." But I tell ye it wis hard work. We had to leave the hoose at six o'clock in the mornin' and walk up the main street in Dalkeith. And Bobby Hogg used to stand where Tom Martin's shop is now—that was Baird the gents' tailor shop then—and he would shout doon at us, "Come on! God dammit tae hell, are ye going to take all mornin' to walk up there?" Well, it wis comin' up the main street in Dalkeith you turned roond by the Buck's Heid and there was a big yard. It's vacant now. But that wis Bobby Hogg's tattie yaird. They called it the Buckie. He used to shout at us, ye ken. So of course we were feared tae loss wir job. If we had went hame and said tae oor mother we got peyed off we would ha' gotten slaughtered. So here we used to hurry up. So we hurried away up the street into the Buckie.[18]

I was born in Dalkeith in Vint's Close, opposite the old Kirk yonder, in September 1909. The Close is all barricaded up now. It all got burned doon. It was tenement buildings in that Close, ye ken, and this woman they cried her Aipple Mary. Well, seemingly, ah dinnae ken what happened—I was just at the school—Aipple Mary set fire tae the buildings. And all the buildings got burned doon. But Aipple Mary went and worked on the

49

farm at Campend—Erskine's Farm at Campend, along by the Sheriffhall way. She worked there for years and years. But she was a loner. She wasnae married, no' that I know of. Of course she was older than me, I dinnae know anything about her history. But that was before the First War.[19]

My father was a miner, an auld miner. I mean they worked in the auld style. Ye ken how the miners worked in these days. The pits werena mechanised in thae days. It was a' hard graft, ye know, pick and shovel. And they had tae walk tae their work, there wis nae transport for them. It wis away ower Millerhill wey—I believe it was Danderhall way.

But then ma faither left the pits and he worked away up at Glencoe, making the big road up at Glencoe, the big tunnel road or somethin' they called it. Ma faither was up there for a long time. And he yaised tae send me money to get a pair o' tackety bits for ma work, sparable bits. I wis only fifteen at that time.[20]

I never seen my grandfather, my father's father, he was dead. But I stayed wi' ma grannie for a period. Auld Phemie Watson was her name. She had only one eye, ye know. And I stayed wi' her, oh, just for aboot three or four months when I was only aboot fourteen or fifteen. She would say, "Here, take the joug and gaun ower to Forester the pub and intae the joug bar and get a sixpence worth o' beer." Well, I used to gaun intae the joug bar with this joug—sixpence worth o' beer for ma grannie, ye ken. But that wis what we had tae dae. It wis just ordinary beer. She had that, well, no' every day but three days oot o' six anyway. I couldnae tell ye what auld Phemie had done for work when she was young.

My mother and father were both born in Dalkeith.

Mrs Agnes Tod, née Douglas, in 1916, aged 21. *c 19963*.

Mrs Agnes Tod in her latter years, shortly before her death in 1988. *c 19967*.

Belle Lindsay, née Reid, c.1917. *c 19964*.

Belle Lindsay with her late sister Maggie at Carrington, c.1970. *c 19962*.

Andrew and Annie Dodds, June 1938, taking afternoon tea outside the house. The teapot is being kept warm by a tea-cosy.

A group of farmworkers at Hilltown Farm, date unknown (pre-1914?). Two of the women wear 'uglies' on their heads, shading both the face and the nape of the neck.

Ruth Walker, 1989.

Jessie Landells, 1989.

But I don't know what ma mother done afore she was married. She never ever spoke aboot it, ye know. Her mother, Grannie Ward, was alive when I was jist a wee lassie at the school, ma grannie but no' ma granda. I dinna ken if granda Ward had been a miner.

Ma grannie Ward she sold the papers on the Sunday. There were a fountain in Dalkeith, opposite the Ship Inn in the middle of the street, and ma grannie Ward used to send the laddies up to the fountain to the bus stop to collect the *News of the World* and the *Sunday Post* and a' that. They took it to her hoose. So thir laddies used to come to the hoose wi' the papers. And this man used to gie her a hand to distribute the papers to the laddies. They had to walk to Pethheid wi' the papers and Whitecraigs, and away by Gilmerton way. She worked from the house. She lived in The Wicket. The Wicket is away now. It's a' Jarnac Court now, ye ken.[21]

I had a sister and a brother. I was the oldest o' the family, two-and-a-half years older than my sister. Ma brother was the youngest. He wid be aboot four years younger than me. But ma brother died—he died away up in England. Henry was his name. But he was in the army and he contacted somethin' wrong wi' his lung. So I think he got discharged oot of the army. But eventually it made up on him and he died.

I went to the Burgh School in Dalkeith. I wisnae a scholar. I left the school at fourteen. You lost all your mates once you left the school, ye know, because they all took up different occupations. They didnae a' go tae the tattie fields.

My first job I worked at Melville Grange. It was a farm, Peter Muirhead's farm at that time. It's not now but it was then. And it wisnae a tattie ferm, it was plants, cabbage plants, Brussels sproot plants.[22] Well, this woman Lizzie Baxter—she's dead now—she said, "Come on, Jess, up to Muirheid's and you'll get a job at the plants aside me. So here we gauns intae Muirheid's and we had tae get on wir knees. Well, you all pulled the plants in front of you. You could put a bunch in your hand. You had to get twenty-five bunches o' these plants a' at your back. Well, there was a woman at the back, she got twenty-five bunches and tied them up wi' string. They were ready for transport. So I used to pu' the plants, well, I was quick with the hands, ye ken. And pull frae here up tae there, the plants in front o' me, withoot moving. Then I would jump up. So Peter Muirheid christened me Rabbit. He said, "Jess, you're like a rabbit." I says, "How? I'm no' eatin' the plants, sir." "No, but," he says, "you're jumping up there like a big patch in front of you." It was a laugh! Oh, I wis a keen worker, oh, aye.

The wages at Melville Grange were aboot 2/3d a day, I think. That would be about 1924. Ye worked five-and-a-half days a week, Saturday morning. I was there just for a wee while. Then that's when I went to Hoggie.

He was a tattie merchant, Bobby Hogg. He got a' his work from the farmers, different farmers, ye know, oh, a' around Dalkeith and further afield than Dalkeith. Wi' Hoggie we had to walk up to our work. We never got transport, no' at that time when we first started. We had to walk to the Duke of Buccleuch's estate, down the Musselburgh road, or doon tae Whitecraigs where the big tattie field would be, or over the Millerhill direction tae Erskine's farm in the fields there. We went to Pethheid, but we had to walk to Pethheid. Then we had tae walk hame again at night.[23]

We had tae get up at five o'clock in the morning. We started in the Buckie at six, ye ken. And this big lorry was standin' in the Buckie wi' about ten or twelve or up to fifteen ton o' tatties on it, in the canvas tattie bags. Ye ken, I wis like a skinned rabbit. I wis only fifteen year auld. I wisna fed tae cairry thur big bags of tatties. An' they were hundredweight bags. The lorry was a' loaded up, ye see. Hoggie wanted them stacked up in a garret place, in the loft. Well, they put a bag on oor back and we had tae climb up thir widden stairs intae the big sheds up the stair and load them a' up there in the shed, ye ken, hinging on tae the banister wi' yin hand and haudin' a bag wi' the other and yer knees knockin' like this gaun up thir widden stairs. So efter we din that we had tae gaun tae oor work in the fields.

And mind ye, there were nae transport tae take us tae oor work. We had tae walk. As I say, we've had to walk to Millerhill tae the ferms, Wellington ferm. And we had to walk doon to the hame ferm doon the Musselburgh road, in tae the home farm afore ye come forrit to Whitecraigs. We went in thir big widden gates, ye ken. And ye had aboot two mile to walk when ye got intae the Duke of Buccleuch's estate tae git tae the tattie pits.

The tattie pits were made ootside with cley and straw. The tattie pits is after the tattie liftin'. That would be aboot the winter, ye ken. And the sna', the sna' and ice on top of them—we had a' that tae take off. We had to strip thir pits so far wi' the cley—a shovel and a graip tae take a' the muck off. And that wis hard work, ye ken. And then we had tae take the straw off and bag it away ower and then start workin' on the tattie pits. Ye didnae go tae the pits in the summer time. The pits were made for winter work.

We a' got wir turn on the different jobs at the pits. One was on the riddle. One was on the scree. That's where a' the brock and the wee tatties fell through the riddle and they slid doon this scree, ye ken. It wis a roon hand riddle and you rattled it off this scree bars and a' the dirt fell doon through. The scree was just like an apparatus, a square metal thing and it had a wee narrow bar on it. Well, we ca'ed a' the rubbish oot the tatties wi' the riddle and it fell doon on the scree and that we put in the brock bags.

That was just for feedin' the pigs, the brock. The wee yins and the cut yins and the rubbish tatties a' fell. They didnae go intae the pigs, they were flung oot.

And then we got a turn sewing the bag. When the tattie bag was fu' we had to take wir turn. We had a needle and string and we had to sew the bags.

We were out in the open a' the time. Cold! We had tae take wir bits off and put straw inside oor bits tae try and keep our feet warm, ye ken.

We din the riddling in the winter time. Then in the month of Mairch, Mairch or April, we were putten on the tattie plantin'. There wis aboot eight or nine o' us a' worked for Bobby Hogg: Hoggie's Angels. You say, "Aye, Jessie, you were a Hoggie's Angel." I says, "I ken."

There wis some o' them aulder than me, in fact most o' them were aulder. There wis an auld woman there, Minnie, Auld Minnie. Oh, she wis aboot sixty-odds. She liked her wee drink, her wee dram an' that, ye ken. And she smoked a pipe. I think it was Minnie McLennan they cried her. She lived hersel. I dinna ken if she wis ever

54

married. She steyed in Baker's Land, the back end o' where Woolworth's back yaird is now.[24] Oh, Minnie's dead years and years ago.

I steyed wi' ma grannie for a wee period in Baker's Land. Baker's Land was opposite the close and Johnston the pawn shop he wis next tae it. We used to take the poker and tongs up tae Johnston the pawn shop, tae get half a croon! Or even ta'en oor weddin' rings up, ye ken, as years went on.[25]

Monday was the day we went tae the pawn shop. If we went up wi' anythin' else we didna want the neighbours see us gaun—we used to put it under oor jaicket. Ah've seen folk—toffs from Eskbank—gaun in wi' their fur coat on.[26] Ah, but they came oot without the fur coat and oot wi' a rain coat. Their fur coat wis ower the counter, ye ken. An' ye ken I had this wee wristlet watch an' it wisnae gaun. Oh, and I wis desperate for money. I said, "Oh, well, Jessie, there's only one thing you've got for the pawn an' that's that wee watch." And I said, "Now I'll hae tae try and shake it and make it gaun." So when I came tae Johnston's pawn shop I looked at the Store clock away ower for the time. I think it wis aboot five past or ten past eleven or somethin'. An' shaking the watch and winding it up, I rushes in. "Mr Johnston." I told him a lie. "Mr Johnston," I says, "I'm gaun tae a dance on Friday so I'll hae tae lift this watch on Friday mornin'." It wis a lot o' lies, ye ken—jist onythin' to get the money. He says, "Well." "Could I get fifteen shillins, please?" "Yes." I couldnae get oot that pawn shop quicker. I never lifted it again—it wis an auld broken thing, ye ken! I never went back tae lift it.

Well, Johnston felt sorry for people. He knew they widnae be there if they didna need the money—ye ken whit I mean. He wisnae a hard, graspin' man but if he could cut you doon a couple of shillins he would cut you doon. In the shop he had a lassie, Bella. I dinna ken her second name. She lived in Back Street, that's St Andrew Street, away at the fit o' Dalkeith. And there wis another, Lizzie Burnett. I went tae the school with that Lizzie Burnett. She had a baby tae Johnston the pawn shop. She wis a single lassie but she worked in the shop, ye know. But right enough he maintained the baby. But I don't know what happened, whether it grew up.

Johnston was a middle-aged man. He wis stocky built. I dinnae ken what he had done before he became a pawnbroker. But he lived in Eskbank, I take it it would be a big house. Then he had another shop in the main street in Dalkeith. They called it the Little Wonder. It's away now. That's where Jarnac Court is, on the main street.

He had a son, a sort o'—there wis something wrong wi' the laddie. Aye, but the laddie used to go in the shop tae. But the faither jist used tae let him dae away. He hadnae his faculties aboot him. We never peyed much attention to that, we were too young to think aboot how awkward it could be.

My grannie Ward steyed in The Wicket. There yist to be lodgin' hooses doon there tae. If we wanted to go to the pawn shop when we were at the school Johnston wouldna take anythin' off the school bairns – you werenae allowed to go in. So we had to gaun up this wee close. This woman steyed up the close. She was deaf and dumb—Dummy Jones they cried her. Well, we had to get her tae take in what we had to pawn. But she took a shillin' or two shillings off everythin' that she took in. That was her payment. I'm no' sayin' she would get mair from the pawn than we would hae done, but she was eligible to take things in where we were too young to go into the pawn shop, ye ken.

Oh, the pawn was busy, och aye! We used to take the poker and tongs oot the fireplace up to Johnston the pawn shop and my faither's suit o' claes. You would get things out on the Friday for the week-end and then put them back in again on the Monday. That was a regular weekly thing. Efter I got married I mind yin time I took ma man's suit of claes up tae the pawn and I think I got £2 on the suit of claes. But here I couldnae lift them again on the Seturday to let ma man oot. So here ma man's hinging oot the windae on the main street and he had a shirt on and a collar and tie, ye ken, and jist his underpants. And his pals were shouting, "Come on. We're gaun for a pint." "You just go doon," he says, "I'll be doon in half an hoor." He couldnae get oot!

When I first started work at Dalkeith there were a lot o' men in lodgin' hooses. Ma uncle Andrew used to be a deputy in Reynolds' lodgin' hoose. He was head of the lodgin' house. He had tae see that the bilers were going and the water was hot an' tae look efter things. I didna ken the folk that lived in the lodgin' hooses but it was mostly men. There were three lodgin' hooses. There were Reynolds', opposite Johnston the pawn shop. Then there was a lodging hoose they called it Black's lodging hoose, but it wis jist a' for men. Then roond the corner, doon The Wicket, where the other door of the pawn shop wis, where you took a' yer parcels and that tae get money for them, there wis a big lodgin' hoose opposite there. But that wis all men tae. In Reynolds' lodgin' hoose I think there were women but very few. I dinnae ken what the women did that lived in these lodgin' hooses.[27]

When there wis nae work on the fields wi Hoggie we had to patch thae tattie bags, put the ones that were torn aside and then we had to patch thae.

How I got the job with Hogg, well, it was a known thing. If ye went up and asked a job he was gled tae take ye. I went up tae the office, ye ken.

We didnae get much wages. We only got aboot eighteen or nineteen shillings a week. We worked for that, say, fae seven o'clock in the mornin' tae five at night. We got ten minutes for wur breakfast, an hoor for wur denner and we got about five minutes or ten minutes at three o'clock.

But we got up at five in the mornin', walked tae the yaird. Ye had to be at the yard at six in the mornin', say quarter past six, and then walked tae the field or tattie pit where ye were workin'. Oh, ye could walk miles afore ye started yer work. And ye couldnae malinger on the road, there wur no malingering.

But as time went on Hogg got the transport. We used to get the big lorry, the tattie lorry, if we were gaun tae the tattie dressin', the tattie pits. Well, the barrels and the weight for weighing the tatties—it was a machine for weighing the tatties—the graips and the shovels and big bundles o' bags and the scree was a' putten on this lorry—nae sides on the lorry or nothin'—and we were clapped on the top o' a' that machinery, gaun away up to Pethheid. It was cauld in the winter time, ken what I mean, an' we were hangin' on like grim death. There was nothin' tae grip on—just the barrels and the machine. There wur no comfort in your travelling.

The barrels were for the tattie lifting. He needed the barrels in the winter time. When we lifted the tatties we put them in oor brat, the coarse apron thing-wied roond ye. Ye buckled it roond and ye gethered wi' yin hand, ye ken, filled your apron. Then ye went an' emptied it intae the barrel. It was the big tatties only that went in the barrel.

There was a barrel on every stent, and there was a wuman on every stent.[28] Then they emptied the barrels into bags—oot the barrel intae bags in the field. They put them into barrels just to judge the hundredweights. But that was the style then. Well, say there wur aboot fifteen barrels in the field in a raw. There wur two wumen came—a wuman at yin side o' the barrel wi' a tattie bag, a wuman on the other side, and they emptied the barrel intae the bag. Then there was a wuman came and she sewed the bags up wi' the string and a big needle.

But then when the lorries came into the field for a load o' tatties in the efternin at fower o'clock we had to load the lorry wi' the bags o' tatties. A wuman at each end o' the bag, and lift it up on tae the lorry, tae aboot ten or fifteen ton o' tatties on the lorry. We had to load them – hundredweight bags. Well, it was as quick as ye could get on wi' it. There wur nae malingering. It was heavy work. I've got a slipped disc. Well, as the years went on – I didnae take it at the time, I just took it when I came up here tae Mayfield tae live. Oh, the work was a terrible strain on the backs o' young lassies! And I mean there wur nothing o' us. We were jist skin and bone 'cause we didnae get fed fur to be robust, ye ken.

Before ye left the hoose ye had just a cup o' tea and a piece on margarine—there wur nae butter then. Well, ye started at seven o'clock in the mornin' and ye got ten minutes for your breakfast, about nine o'clock—oh, just sit in the field. Two slices o' jam bread. I got that for years. And four slice o' jam bread for my piece at dinner time. An' we got a cup o' tea. He used to send me to the ferm for tae get the pitchers filled up wi' the hot water fae the farm houses. Oh, we aye got hot tea.

We got an oor for wur denner at twelve o'clock. We just had it in the field. If it was wet, well, if ye were near the ferm ye just went to the ferm. If ye werenae near the ferm and it was wet we just sheltered under the trees. There wur aye wids. See, the tattie pits were made ootside—they were a' built ootside, and we had to work ootside. But when it came on rain or that we just went intae the wid and sheltered, a tattie bag ower wur heid. We made it like a hood thing and pit it ower wur heid.

Ye went back tae work after your denner at one o'clock and then ye got aboot ten minutes' break in the efternin, just for a cup o' tea or just tae go for a . . ., ye ken. Then oo finished at five o'clock and came hame. I was hame aboot six o'clock. It depended on the distance. Oh, that wis a long day, wis it no'! I mean, up fae five in the mornin'.

And when oo came hame we used tae get wir denner – supposed to be wir denner—a slice o' sliced sausage and half an egg and a slice o' breid. We used to say to ma mother—ma mother was a demon—I'd say, "Mother, is it a'right—can I get another slice o' bread, please?" Tae beg! "Can I get another slice o' bread, please?'

And, ye see, wi' workin' ootside in the field, when ye came in it made ye drowsy.

Efter we got wur dinner we'd the hoosework tae dae. Helped ma mother? She din nothin'. And then on the Tuesday we'd tae get intae the wash-hoose, kin'le the fire in this big auld hoose. Kin'le the fire wi' sticks and

60

coal and pit the washin' pot on the top o' the fire tae
heat the water, tae gie us hot water tae dae the washin'.
That was on a Tuesday.

Ma mother and ma faither was separated. Ma faither
was away at Glencoe. But he used tae write tae me—I
was his favourite, ye see. He used tae write tae me. And
ma mother wid say to me, "Write 'im a letter and tell 'im
ye're needin' a new pair o' bits"—which was a lot o' lies.
This was fur her tae get the money. So I used tae write
tae ma faither. I hated every word I put on the paper, ye
ken, fur I knew it was a lie. I mean, I would rather have
the truth, no matter how bad it may be, as a liar. So ma
faither used tae send me aboot £5. Ma faither was a hard
worker, ye see. So that wis £5 tae ma mother. £1 was a
lot o' money then, ye ken.

So when I wis at Hoggie's, on the Tuesday we used
tae go up tae the office fur sub—five shillins sub off oor
wages. And we went up on the Thursday night also—
five shillins sub. That was ten shillins away off eighteen
shillins. So I hadnae much pey tae get on the Seterday
mornin'.

Hoggie didnae charge interest on the sub. He writ it a'
doon, what ye got and how much ye got and how often
ye got it. Oh, a' the girls did that, they a' went for subs.
Things wur hard, it wis the only way tae keep goin', tae
get a sub.

When we first started we jist went oot tae the fields wi'
oor skirts and a peeny, an auld-fashioned peeny on the
top an' that, ye ken. We put a sack roond aboot us. You
were tryin' tae keep yer claes that you had in below clean.
And if it came on rain we jist put a sack ower oor heid.
We jist wore a heidsquare. Well, sometimes we wore a
heidsquare, sometimes we didnae, ye ken. In the winter

time you'd to put a scarf on and gloves. I had sparable bits. And you used tae take them off and pit straw inside tae keep your feet warm till ye got hame, ye ken. Oh, many days we wur cold!

Well, when we got intae the hoose, efter we got wur denner an' oor jobs started an' that, I've seen us sittin' and jist drowsing. And afore ye kent where ye were ye were quickly brought up—quickly wakened. My mother yist tae slap us across the face: "Get on! Get the fireside din!" So we didnae get time to sleep.

I wasnae married when I worked at Hoggie's. When I got married I gave up work then.

Hogg was a wee man and he had his office in the yaird. And this wuman she was employed in his office. Annie May Thorburn was her name, from Dalkeith. And she run a' the business in Bobby Hogg's office. She paid a' the bills. He never bothered, he left it a' to her. She was a kind o' clerkess, office manager. She was aulder than me. But she was a slim person. She didnae look her years. But she was aulder than me—she would hae to be to be in that job. She never married.

Bobby Hogg lived away up Eskbank, I dinnae ken where but up in Eskbank.[29] He never gave his wife any money. She had to come down to the office and ask Annie May Thorburn for money for to get messages. And she also had to bring back the change and hand it over to Annie May Thorburn. Annie had a' the say o' the cash, you know. Oh, Bobby Hogg was a skinflint, he was, he was.

But he had a nephew, cried Jimmy Hogg. Jimmy worked in the yard an' a'. But Jimmy was a hell of a nice person, ye ken what I mean. You could come and go wi' Jimmy but you were feared tae talk to Bobby 'cause he would eat the heid off ye. He was very alert. He knew the business a'right, ye ken. Och, he was aulder than us. He would be aboot in his fifties anyway.

As I say, I was born in Vint's Close. My mother and father lived in a room there. I dinnae mind nothing about that place because we shifted tae Amos Close. They called it the Dub—Dublin Close. I dinnae ken why they cried it that but that's what they used to say, the Dub Close. Well, that was just a wee room and kitchen, the ground floor.

At Amos Close there were three people lived in that lobby. Ma mother was a ground flat, a woman abune us and a woman above that again. An' they got their turn o' the wash hoose in the close, and then ye could jist go in to the wash hoose as ye wanted. Coming intae the close ye passed about four houses then this auld sort o' demolished hoose but they ta'en it for the wash hoose. That was the wash hoose, then there was my mother's hoose. Then opposite my mother there was this big yard. It was a dairy—Allan the dairy. He had coos and hens an' ye used to buy the milk from him and the eggs, and the hens used to come oot the yird on to the close, ye ken, run aboot the close. Of course, there wis nae roof on the close, ye ken, it wis jist open. And the coos used to come in the back intae the yird, ye ken, come right through the close. I used to love that. I've always had a great love for horses and the coos.

Oor hoose had inside water and the auld-fashioned grate, the oven beside it, and a square metal thing that slid under the fire. We'd a' that to clean—it was a lot o' work.

At Amos Close my mother slept in the livin' room. Ma faither was away—they'd parted when I was quite young. Well, we'd a' to sleep in the one room, my sister, brother an' me, but there were two beds in the one room: one there and one there. My brother hae got a bed to hissel'. An' my mother had a bed in the livin' room. The livin' room wasnae situated fur a bed, ken what I mean, but it was there. Ye walked in the main door o' the living room and ye were walkin' intae the bed. There wurnae that much space. Well, that was the position until I left tae get married.

The sink was in the kitchen. There was a toilet in the house, it was just a wee box thing. You came out the livin' room and the toilet was there. There was no bath, no, oh, no. Well, my sister yaist to wash ma back and I yaist to wash hers. It was a basin, we used to ca' it a bath in the basin—a big zinc basin, ye ken. Of course we never got a bath through the week. It was aye at the week-end we got it. There were no town baths in Dalkeith then.

I dinnae ken if my friends had the same conditions. I wasnae one for runnin' aboot the hooses. I mean, everybody had too much tae dae theirsel', ye ken what I mean. But I'll tell ye I used to see ma friends when I went to the dancin' at the week-end. I used to go to the Drill Hall in Dalkeith. That's where Jarnac Court is now—opposite the auld post office. Oh, I used to love dancing. I've aye been a guid dancer up until recently. We used to get half-a-crown pocket money. My mother used to say, "Now, you'd better be in by twelve o'clock the night." She allowed us tae twelve on a Saturday and on a Sunday ye had to be in at nine o'clock. And if we were ten minutes late we got battered useless—kept in for six weeks and nae pocket money. One Sunday I was oot in the street and thur fellaes came doon fae

Nittengrange. They used tae walk frae Nittengrange to see the Dalkeith lassies, ye ken. And I'm standin' along wi' ma pal Teenie Morgan. We're standin' and the polis came and he took wir name and address and we got charged for maloiterin' on the pavement. I got slaughtered when I went hame. That wis me in for another six weeks, nae pocket money.

What we wore through the week we had to wear on the Seterday and the Sunday. But we tried tae keep somethin' guid for the dancin' at night, ye ken what I mean. So the claes—this wuman used tae come frae Edinburgh, Mrs Shaw, wi' a pack on her back. And ye used to get things for threepence or tuppence and sixpence, a' second-handed claes. An', oh, I wis skin and bone at that time, ye ken, a wee garment fitted me. Mrs Shaw came every Seterday and the folk in the Close—Amos Close—she opened her pack ootside and they a' swarmed roond about it, grabbing fur the best thing that wis in the pack. What ye'd dae to be braw dressed! I'll no' say everybody in Dalkeith got dressed that way—but the folk in the Close did.

We didnae get time tae read. An' we didnae get any papers—my mother wouldna buy them. But we hadnae time. When ye came in ye were tired and ye had a' this hoose work tae dae. Once in a blue moon—every time there were Charlie Chaplin films an' a' that, ye ken, we went tae the picture house in Dalkeith. I think it was sixpence to get intae the pictures. We used to sell jeely jars, lemonade bottles, to get money. The picture house was where Jarnac Court is now—yon big building opposite, goin' up the steps, that was the picture house. There were two picture hooses. There was that yin and there was one they cried it the Palais or something—

a wee picture house, where Eskdaill Court is. Aw, we didnae go often, just once a week.[30]

After I got married I lived in Donaldson's Close. It was a room and kitchen, a ground-floor house. You had to go right through oot ma living room to get intae the bedroom. But it was a big bedroom like ma living room. And, oh, the clockers—beetles! Across the flair—I was terrified. Oh, and the bugs up the wa', wee broon things that live in the buildings. They were all over the walls. And the grass used tae be up through the flair in the room. They were auld, auld hooses. But I lived there, efter I got married I lived there.

I went to Edinburgh in 1941 and first of all I worked in the Chimes Hotel, Royal Terrace. Then I worked in Younger's brewery. And I worked in Craigmillar laundry. But I didnae like it there. I was just aboot two months there, I think. And I worked in a biscuit factory an' a', McFarlanes.

But, oh, I liked the fields. Mind ye, the tattie field's back-breakin'. When I come up here tae Mayfield to live in 1954 I got a job wi' Alex Denholm from Musselburgh. He had the big sheds doon at Musselburgh opposite the sea—Fisherrow. So I was claimed right away tae go to the tattie fields because I had the experience. The wuman that came for me, that was Mrs Nellie Young from the Bryans.[31] She was in charge o' the squad wi' Alex Denholm o' Musselburgh. He was the potato merchant in Musselburgh, and vegetables an' a'. So Nellie came up. She says, "Jessie," she says, "what aboot comin' oot tae the tatties?" I says, "Oh, well, I wouldnae mind." So I started wi' Denholm.

And that was only aboot 3/6d a day, I think it wis. We got the lorry oot there at seven o'clock in the mornin'—

he'd the lorry wi' the canopy on it fur us, ye see. Oh, they were catered for better then, ye ken. Of course ye were more advanced as the times went on. So here I used to get the lorry oot there and I got dropped off there at night an' a'. But Denholm was a'right, ye ken.

We worked round the area. We've been away at Gifford—worked at Gifford—and we were at Muirton, East Fortune. I've worked doon at East Fortune. It wis Midlothian and East Lothian. We didnae go to the Borders, oh, no, no' as far away as that. But we went away, oh, miles and miles past Pethheid. I think it was Garvald they cried it. It was a monastery away at the top – Nunraw. I went there. We were in the sheds workin' at that time.

They never had a union at the tatties. But I'll tell you when I was on the tatties, we were only getting I think it was fower shillings a day at this time, wi' Denholm. This wis when I wis up here at Mayfield. So here, they were all gaun tae come oot on strike. They wanted an extra sixpence, an' they widnae gie us it. So we said, "We're coming oot on strike. We're not going to work." So we a' stopped. That wis at the tattie liftin' at the time. It was hard work, ye ken, at the tattie liftin'. Ye didnae jist gather yer tatties off the digger, there was a harrows came at the back of it. And it used to bring up tatties, ye know. Where a' the tatties came frae! Ye thought ye were gatherin' yer stent awfy clean. Ken, I hated a dirty stent. An' ye were getherin' yer tatties an' ye were fair away with yersel. When the harrows came along— nae tatties. But there wis as many tatties lying after the harrows as when the digger ca'ed them oot!

So here, we said we were comin' oot on strike. So we downed tools. And the boss came on the field. An' he says, "What's this?" We said, "We're wantin' a rise, sixpence o' a rise. We're no' bein' paid equivalent tae what we were working for." "You'll get nae rise here," he says. "Ye're not gettin' a sixpence. If ye're not satisfied ye know what to do." We said, "Aye— we'll dae it. In the lorry an' we're gaun hame." He says, "Ye cannae dae that. If you're comin' oot on strike," he says, "you'll walk home." Oo says, "No, we'll no'. We'll no' walk. You brought us here wi' transport. You'll take us back wi' transport." So Nellie Young—she was the chargehand—she says, "Aye, we're wantin' a sixpence rise." "Well," he says, "Nellie, you should know better." She says, "No, ah'm jist like everybody else."

Even the women, them that was on emptying the barrels every day, they came oot on strike an' a'. An' he says tae them as well, "Ye're wanting a sixpence rise. Ye're no' gettin' it, ye're no' gettin' it." So eventually efter aboot an hoor's loss of work an' the yappin' that a' went on frae him, he agreed. He said, "I'll gie ye thruppence." Oo says, "Naw, we're no' wantin' thruppence, we're wantin' sixpence." See, that gave us 4/6d. We were wantin' sixpence. So he hummed and he hawed. It wis like tearing the hert oot o' him tae gie us sixpence—an' the money he wis makin'! An' ye were only allowed a bilin o' tatties at night. Well, some places oo went the fermer wouldnae allow ye tae take a bilin' off his fields. Well, a bilin' was as much as ye could take, if ye could get away with it. But ye're restricted wi' some o' the fermers, ye see—they're awful mean.

So he says, "Right, I'll gie the sixpence. But I'll tell ye something tae. Ye'll get more than a sixpence," he says, "for I'll tell ye what ah'm gaun tae dae. There will be no stoppin' at the shops in the mornin' tae get yer biscuits and chocolates and fags. If you get sixpence you'll be here earlier in the fields. There'll be nae stoppin' for quarter an hoor at the shops in the mornin'." And so he did!

But here we sorted him. That stopped for aboot three mornings. So oo says tae the driver, "Here ye'll hae to stop and let us in tae the shop. Ah've nae breid. The shop had nae breid yesterday." This was a lie! So we started again stoppin' at the shops in the mornin'. So that wis when I worked wi' Denholm. It was 4/6d a day we got.

When I left Denholm's I went tae a Glesgae firm but the contracts were here. Tony Lovell wis the gaffer. He lived in Dalkeith, further doon a wee bit frae the Masons Arms.[32] He died just aboot two years ago. He wis a wee man. Martha was his wife. They were Irish. Oh, she wis a' for the firm, that firm from Glescae, Fulton's. That wis the contract wi' them. Tony wis the gaffer. The man at the scheme he wis the contractor for the firm. He got Tony Lovell—him and Martha—tae get the workers.

So Tony used to send the van up for us. We got it oot there. So we were taken doon tae Dalkeith efter we were on the van from here. Oh, there were about twelve or fifteen of us, ye ken. They came from Birkenside. He went up tae Birkenside tae collect them: Mary Kerr and Belle Brazally and Chrissie Jamieson and Ina Jamieson and Margaret Jamieson. They were sisters, ye see.[33]

Oh, there were men tae. They took men at the tattie liftin' when the tatties were more plentiful and they needed orders. They got men. There wis a wee man and he kep' us gaun wi' the bags. It was paper bags then, ye ken, whit they are in now. And the rest of the men they helped tae empty the barrels an' that and load the lorries.

So this Teresa Wylie, she belanged Widburn at one time but she got married and she went tae live up at Arniston, in the Store Cottages.[34] I think it wis the Store Cottages ye cried it. She's dead now. So she was a thrifty cratur, ye ken. And when they got intae Dalkeith, she aye went to the shop in the morning for her cigarettes. And she was mean, dead mean. I says, "Theresa, will ye dae me a favour, hen?" She says, "What is it, Jess?" I said, "Get me a quarter of Daylight Roses." There wisnae such a thing! I said, "Get me a quarter of Daylight Roses." This wis jist a gimmick.

So she wis in the shop for aboot half an hoor. Tony the gaffer used to say: "Where's that bloody woman away tae?" I says, "She's at the shop, Tony." "I'll shop her when she comes back!" So Theresa comes oot the shop. "Jessie Landells," she says, "there's no' such a thing as Daylight Roses. The man had a' the shop turned oot. He was looking for Daylight Roses. There werenae such a thing." "Oh," ah said, "ye should jist have got Elephant's Tiptaes!" She said, "I'll kill ye when I come in that van!" I said, "So ye will!" We got laughs. Aye we did. So Tony stopped the shop racket.

When I was working wi' Fulton's the Glesgae tattie merchant, and Tony Lovell was the gaffer, when the tatties werenae ready to be lifted, he put us on to the leeks doon at the market gardens in Musselburgh, away at the back o' Millerhill. There wur big fields o' leeks. We'd to pull the leeks and skin them, fill the boxes, cairry them ower, put them on this widden contraption, and Martha and her man Tony—that was the Irish couple I worked wi'—they weighed them and pit them intae bundles for the shops or to go to the market.

There were Irish with Fulton's squad, but Bobby Hogg

never employed Irish people. But when the Irish people came here they lived in the bothy up at D'Arcy. They lived there and they just a' fed through one another, ye ken whit I mean? One made the grub and the rest a' just sat doon, ken.[35]

The Irish were men and women, no children, jist adults. They stayed up there at D'Arcy for years. It's no' a bothy now, it's a bought house now. It has all been modernised. There were three bothies there. it was just all the one batch, ye know. There were three different doors. That was since I came up here to Mayfield in 1954. Of course they were maybe up there before I came here.

But when I went doon tae Aberlady tae work, we worked on the ferm dressin' tatties an' a' that, ye see. We were a' on the planter at the tattie machine, plantin' tatties with the machines. But when they were sortin' the machine we had tae clean up the ferm. So here there wis four o' us sittin' on the machine, a box of tatties each side of ye, in front o' ye, and the wee cups that you put the tatties in and it revolved roond. Oh, this man the fermer of the ferm, he didnae like me. Every chance he got he used to pick. I used to say, "Here, sir, if ah get any mair o' your sarcasm the tatties are not gaun tae gaun in the machine—you're gaun tae gaun in the machine." I says, "Look, I dinna have tae belittle masel tae ye. I can work anywhere." I says, "Ye maybe dinna like ma face but I like yours less. So close your mouth or I'll close it for ye." An' he never said another word efter that. That was him. That was a sprag pit in his wheel. But, I'll tell ye, the fermers were nice enough as long as ye were daein' yer work, ye ken. But this man was never satisfied. He was a right grab and he hadnae a nice way

of talkin', ye know—a very sarcastic and an abrupt way
of talking. An' I couldna stand that.

But, oh, the fields were my work. Ye see when I
worked in the fields? I'm no' jokin' an' ah'm no' braggin'
but I was one of the brawest women up here in Mayfield
— no' good looking, but I had a tan, I was bronzed wi' the
sea air. Healthy! Oh, I wis. Oh, I loved the open air.

When I worked wi' Denholm, we used to start at seven
o'clock in the morning in the summer time. But here we
were working doon at Whitecraigs at the tatties—tattie
lifting, ye see. And ye ken there were hooses doon at the
foot of the tattie field. Well, every mornin' we stripped.
So here I used to go to the woman for hot water for oor
tea. Well, she started giein' me a cup o' tea and a biscuit
in the hoose. An' ah wis slippin' her doon a few tatties
on the quiet. But if the gaffer had seen me I would ha'
got my books.

So here this morning, it was kind o' airy so a lot o'
them took their coats off, but I kept mine on. And
the gaffer twigged. See, I wis pickin' up tatties and
I was fillin' my bag for gaun for the tea—tae take
the tatties ower tae this woman. So the gaffer says tae
the forewoman, Nellie Young, "See Jess, she's up tae
something," he says. "Every morning she has her coat
off at seven o'clock, she's one of the first to have her
coat off. And they've a' got their coats off—but Jess has
kept hers on. She's daein' that for a purpose."

So I taen the tatties ower tae the woman and I came
back wi' the tea. John the gaffer says, "Well, Jess, you
would be thinking you were clever, eh?" "Who me?
Naw, I've never been clever, Johnny," I says. "What
bit are ye gettin' at?" "Every morning," he says, "ye
little bugger that ye are," he says, "yer coat's off at

seven o'clock in the mornin'. Now they've a' got their coats off and you're the only yin wi' yer coat on," he says. "You must have kep' it on for a purpose." I says, "Johnny, I just dinnae like takin' my coat off. I dinnae feel like takin' it off." He says, "You know why? Because you were hidin' the tatties that you were taking doon tae that bloody woman," he says. "I seen ye."

But here at this time it was the machines, the tatties a' went on to the machines and it was a revolving wheel, a big belt. It was for carryin' the tatties oot the field. Instead of us hand picking we were put on the machines. The rest of them were at the tattie dressin'. So thir tatties went up to the dresser. So here, jet propelled, this woman says, "Jessie, you can dae this machine yourself." "Aye," I says, "but I'm no'. If I start it masel' I'll get it tae dae." So here I had false teeth, ye see, daein' four on a wee bit plate. And workin' away like blazes ah took a fit only of coughing and my teeth fell oot and went doon the hole. I says, "Johnny, stop the machine, stop the machine!" "What's wrong?" I says, "Just take a look at me, I've nae teeth. I've lost ma teeth in the machine." I didna tell him that there were only four on a wee bit plate. Well, he went wi' the graip. He stopped the machine and they were a' oot looking for ma teeth. And he walked away back to the dreel that had been ca'ed oot, diggin' wi' the graip, thinkin' he had fund ma teeth. They never fund them. But here, this woman on the machine she walked away roond the other side. She says, "Jessie, here's teeth. Is that yours?" I said, "Oh, aye, thank God, Betty, thank God." Johnny the gaffer says, "Now"—he swore—"dinna tell me that's what ye lost. That's what ye got the field in an uproar for—four bloody teeth," he says, "on a wee bit half plate! That's what we've lost half a day's work looking for—thae!" I says, "Johnny, ah couldnae tell ye it was only four, sir." I says, "Ah'm bad wi' them but I'm a damn sight worse wi' them oot, sir!"

I think I worked aboot three or four years in the fields efter I came here tae Mayfield in 1954. I never went tae any inside work. When there wur nae work wi' Denholm, White came doon for me to go tae the threshing mill. It was ootside, ye see, in the fields on the Edgeheid road.[36] I says, "Right, Robin." Robin White was 'is name. So I went up to the mill and we're daein' away. So here I only worked wi' him for aboot two days. I thought I would be there three days but I got notified frae Denholm at Musselburgh to come oot to him. He had work for us, ye see. So I said to my man, "Wullie, I cannae go tae White's the morn," I says, "because I'll hae tae go back to my ain job." Denholm's was more permanent, White's was just a flash in the pan like—three or four days, you know. So I says tae Wullie, "You'd better gaun up an' tell Robin that I've got word for my ain job." But here Wullie never went.

So I went away to Denholm's. But here when I came hame Wullie says, "You've caused some racket wi' White." I says, "No' me." "Well," he says, "White was doon at this door an' the length he went, aboot you no' comin' up there. He's shoutin', 'She's left the damn mill standin' up there, naebody tae work it. We're at a loss', he says, 'she should have come up and telt me.'" I says, "Wullie, you're at fault. I told you to go up and tell White aboot it." "Oh," he says, "Jessie, I couldnae be bothered walking up that road." So here I had tae go up to White's for ma wages. So I gauns up on the Seturday mornin'. "Jessie," he says, "I've a good

74

mind not to pay ye." I says, "Why?" He says, "Ye let me doon. Ye left the damn mill standin'. There wur naebody here tae work it," he says. "Ye left us in a pickle." He says, "Ye could hae came an' telt me." He says, "You'll no' get a job wi' me again." I says, "Aye, I will. I'll bet you I will." He says, "No, you'll no'."

So a wee while efter this I wasnae working again. So White comes doon. He says, "Are you gaun tae come up and work?" I says, "I thought you werenae gaun tae gie me a job." "Come on," he says, "up tae the tattie liftin'." It was just up the Tower Brae there.

At denner time oo sat in the stables to get oor piece and tea, ye see. An' he had a big dug, ca'ed it Kim—a hoose dug. And here yin day I had ma piece in ma bag hingin' on the hedge and his dug came and ate ma piece. So I went tae him. I says to Robin, "Robin, Kim's ate ma piece and I'm left withoot a piece. I'll hae tae go hame for ma denner." "No, no," he says, "go to the hoose an' Mrs White will give you a piece." I says, "Thank you, Robin." So I goes and tells Mrs White the dug ate ma piece. She made up two big slice o' bread—roast beef on it—their own cooking like, no' the roast beef you buy at the shops—and tomataes, and a big slice o' fruit icin' cake. And of course I thought this was great. I'd telt Robin I'd liver and onions on ma ain piece. And I'm tellin' the workers I'd only jam on ma piece. Robin was standin' at the stable door listenin'. I never seen him. "Aye," he says, "ye're daein' fine, Jess." My face went the colour o' . . . ! "Well," I said, "Robin, I've got to kid masel' on some time." He said, "It was only jam you had on your piece." I says, "I ken." Oh, I couldnae go back again.

But when I was wi' White's here he had hens and the

hens used tae run oot and in the wids an' at the back o' the stables. See the hens we stole! I used to say to this fella—White had two or three fellas up there—and this fella used to work wi' a butcher's. Stevie they cried 'im. Efter he was retired fae the butcher I gien 'im a job. I says, "Come on up and get a job at the tattie liftin' beside me." Well, him bein' a butcher ye ken how they can handle the hens. I says, "Get me a hen and I'll gie ye five shillings, Steve." I says, "Wring its neck but dinnae hurt it, son, dinnae hurt it." I said to masel', "It's a dear hen, five shillings." So here he used tae dae a hen in for me and take twa for hissel. White was bound to miss thae hens. So here at denner time instead o' sitting takin' ma denner in the field I ta'en this bag for my piece an' that, and I said to Steve, "You put it in. I cannae touch them, son, you pit it in the bag for me, please." He puts the hen in the bag an' I gauns doon the road. So I laid it in the scullery in oor hoose. So when I went up they were started their work in the field. Robin says, "Where hae you been, Jessie?" I says, "I was at the shops for fags, Robin." Oh, the lies! And the feathers are flying oot the bag, ye ken! He says, "What's a' that in your bag?" I says, "I was cleanin' oot a feather pillae, Robin, I cannae dae wi' feathers. I was cleaning oot this feather pillae, Robin, afore I left hame for," I says, "I hate feathers fleein' aboot the hoose." See the lies! Nae wonder ma soul's black!

So when I came in frae work that night Wullie my man says, "I thought you telt me that ye gien the laddie five shillings to kill the hen?" I says, "So I did." "Well," he says, "it was fu' o' life when it came here. It was flyin' aboot the scullery. I couldnae catch it." Oh, many's a hen I took fae White's up there. But they were a' at it.

I liked the fields. Oh, mind ye, the tattie field's back-breakin'. And ye take yer piece wi' yer dirty hands and everythin'. But it never bothered me any. Oh, I loved every minute workin' in the fields and I loved everybody that worked beside me on the fields, ye ken. Oh, I loved the work. I'm only sorry that I'm too auld for the work now.

One day we went to this ferm, oh, it's a guid bit away – away by where the monastery was, Nunraw, up the hill. And we wur sittin' at the stable. There were stables, wee ponies an' that. This man worked in the stables and I said, "Son, ye no' got an auld horse shoe you can gie me?" I says, "I dinnae want a big ugly thing like masel'," I says, "I'm wantin' a wee horse shoe." So he gien me this wee horse shoe—it's still hangin' oot there. But here he had this minah birds, the talking birds, ye ken. So ma gaffer, Martha, she's sittin' yappin' away. So I says to the bird, "Hello, son, say 'Jessie, where's Jessie?'" It says, "Bugger off."

Mrs Ruth Walker

[Mrs Walker was born, one of a family of five, in Dumfriesshire at Sanquhar in 1923. She spent her childhood there and in Glasgow and Lanarkshire, where her stepfather was a shepherd near Crawfordjohn. Both her mother and grandmother were farm workers. Mrs Walker left school at age fourteen in 1937 and worked for a year on a farm at Crawford in Lanarkshire, hand-milking cows, shawing turnips, turning hay with the rake and carting it, collecting harvest sheaves for binding, making coils (small heaps of hay), and driving a horse and cart to bring the sheaves in. She was up at 4 a.m. seven days a week to milk the cows and didn't get to bed until midnight. She had one Sunday off each month. She also did general domestic work in the farmhouse. The wages were 25 shillings (£1.25p) a month after deductions for her bed and board (she lived in the farmhouse). "Everybody else," she recalls, "was really in the same position."

After a year, aged fifteen, she moved to another farm at Crawford, where she did more housework, but also did milking and harvest work. It was "a much shorter day" from 6 a.m. to 5 p.m.—though again it was seven days a week—and again she lived in the farmhouse. The wages were £18 for six months—i.e. the £18 was paid every six months, with six months' waiting time when she began. She could go home once a fortnight on Sundays.

Mrs Walker remained in that job until 1941 when she was seventeen or eighteen. Her wages and hours remained the same throughout those three years. Her third job was on a farm near Biggar, where she worked mostly in the farmhouse and helped with the milking. The hours were from 6 or 7 a.m. until 5 p.m. She can't now recall what the wages were, but thinks they were "a bit more" than in her second job.

Mrs Walker left that job a year later in 1942 when she got married. Her husband, who was serving in the Royal Air Force, had worked as a miner at Whitehill Colliery, Rosewell, in Midlothian, and she went to live at Rosewell with his parents. There her daughter was born, but Mrs Walker and her husband separated near the end of the War in 1945. She lived with her own parents in Kintyre, Argyllshire, for a year, then got a part-time job on a farm at Lesmahagow in Lanarkshire, milking and doing some farm housework. She moved briefly to a farm near Dunoon with her parents, then to Kilmarnock and from there to Darwen in Lancashire, where she worked for several years in a food factory, then very briefly in cotton spinning mills and a paint factory.

After eight years at Darwen, Mrs Walker returned to Scotland in 1952. By that time her parents were at Ravensneuk farm, Penicuik, where her stepfather was shepherd. Mrs Walker now continues her story in her own words.]

I really came to Ravensneuk for a holiday. My mum and dad had only come the year before. I liked it here and I just asked mum. She says, "If you can get a job you can stay." I mean she was kind of lonely as well. She was on her own a lot because my dad was out all day practically, except at dinner time, seven days a week.

Mr Graham, the farmer, offered me a job on the farm and I just took it. My daughter, who was ten years old, wasnae bothering whether she left England or not. She was quite happy there but she's quite happy up here too. She soon made friends, and she made friends with the farm ones as well. She was forever up at the farm. She went to the High School in Penicuik, it was from primary upwards. She quite liked it. When she left school she was an invisible mender at Caerlee Mill at Innerleithen. She was there for a good few years and then got married and went to live at Tweedsmuir. The chap she married was a shepherd.

My job at Ravensneuk then in 1952 was everything. It was outside all the time. I was working with the cows as well, helping with the machine milking. Mr Graham had a herd of about 36. That was quite large, he hadnae room for any more. It was a dairy farm at that time, well, dairy and arable and he had a few sheep as well. I just can't remember how many acres there were.

I didn't do any domestic work at all in the farmhouse – it was all outside, the cows, the hens. They had hens out in the free range at that time. I didn't do ploughing, I didn't work wi' the horse.

But if there was tractor driving out in the field to do I had to do it, you know, when they were carting. My dad learned us to drive the tractor up in the field up there. Oh, it wasnae too bad, didnae take long! I quite enjoyed it. It was an open tractor, a wee old Ferguson at that time, one o' the wee grey ones. Oh, it was easy going in it, quite easy. There was no protection but I never was out in the wet weather, it was just really in the hay and the harvest time when I was out in it. I wasnae out in it for ploughing or anything like that. My dad did most of the ploughing with it and the horse did some ploughing that was too soft for the tractor. I didn't do any cutting with the tractor either, reaping or cuttin' hay. We just did the carting and building the haystacks and when the corn was brought in helped build the big corn stacks.

There were other workers on the farm too, when I began. There was one ploughman, the byreman, the shepherd (my dad), and the ploughman's wife. She did the milking in the morning and I did it in the afternoon. And of course the boss 'iself, Mr Graham, used to work. The ploughman wasn't a tractorman, he still ploughed with horses at that time. My dad, well, wi' not having so many sheep my dad was tractorman as well. The ploughman was round about the same age as my dad, coming up for sixty then. I don't think he wanted to learn to drive the tractor, he wanted the horses all the time.

There were two horses, Meg and Charlie. The ploughman, John Struth, did all the stable work. He was married and lived in the cottages up the road. They were just single-storey cottages then. The byreman was in one and the ploughman was in the other.

There wasn't any kind of grading among the Ravensneuk farm workers. They were just all in the one category. The shepherd wasn't really seen as the man at the top. The ploughman was there long before my dad came.

When I started my wages was £9-odd a week. That was just the normal wage for a woman agricultural worker then in 1952. That was for about 11½ hours a day, seven days a week. I never knew what wages my dad got as shepherd-tractorman. And I never knew what the ploughman or the byreman got. I never knew—and I never asked. We got our wages paid promptly on the Saturday morning.

I was up aboot five, half five, in the morning. I just had to walk up the road to the farm, it's just round the corner. Sometimes I had something to eat first but when you started at six you had to come down and get your breakfast and go back up again. I came down just after half seven. The time I had for breakfast just depended on when the milking finished and you got the cows out in the summer time.

The byreman was milking. I was carrying the milk and emptying it, putting it through the cooler and filling the 10-gallon cans ready for the lorry to collect. I was assisting the byreman but if he was busy I could change the machines. Just as soon as I was finished breakfast I went back up again to the farm. I ate maybe toast or something like that, I couldnae face bacon at that time in the morning! Then I worked from, say, the back of eight o'clock till twelve. We had an hour for dinner time. I had soup or something like that. I never took a flask of tea up in the morning, not when I had breakfast as late. Then I was back up to the farm at one o'clock. I didnae have anything to eat or drink in the afternoon. The day's work finished at half-past five then I had a cooked tea because my daughter came home shortly after that and I had a cooked meal for her. That was the main meal of my own day as well, just maybe potatoes and meat and maybe a pudding, and soup if I had plenty soup left. When my daughter was still at school she didn't come home at midday, she took a piece with her.

Well, those were the hours I worked at Ravensneuk, for so many years, from six in the morning until half-past five at night. But as the years went on it was five o'clock finish and then maybe a quarter to five—it gradually reduced. But I worked seven days a week. There was a week-end off once every three weeks from Saturday dinner time till Monday morning. That was normal. And then it got down to a week-end off every fortnight.

We got a fortnight's holiday from when I began at Ravensneuk in the early 1950s. If we were goin' anywhere we could ask to get off but we usually just took the holidays when the farmer said we could, because if we wanted July, well, that was hay time. If we wanted August, it was still hay time. August or September, well, that was really harvest time. And, I mean, the other workers they were gettin' their holidays as well. We couldnae all go off at the one time. I think the ploughman he said when he wanted his holidays because, well, his two children were at school. They were older than my daughter Margaret who was at school then too but I didnae really want any holidays when she was at school. I didnae want to take her away from school. The ploughman didnae mind taking his children from the school for his holidays. I took my holidays just if we happened to be at a slack time, maybe in between July or August. But I didn't go away, oh, no, maybe for a day here and there. The other farm workers did that too.

I was never in a union in any of my jobs. Well, I never was asked really. Down in England I was in the Transport & General Workers' Union, when I was in the factory. But not when I was on the farm. I can't remember anybody at all in Lanarkshire or in

Midlothian who was in a farmworkers' union. Nobody ever asked us to join a union or anything like that. I don't think the byreman ever was in a union either, nor the ploughman; and my dad was never in a union. I never heard him saying he was payin' union dues or anything like that. The union must have been very weak wherever we were.

We just worked away and then when it came through that we were gettin' less hours or more wages or that, we just took it as granted. We didnae confab or anything about it. I never heard the other workers asking Mr Graham the farmer to reduce hours or anything like that. Relations between us workers and Mr Graham were quite friendly. We worked together in the fields. He did a bit of the ploughing. We never had any sense that we were being put upon in any way, oh, he was a good boss. I'll give him his due, he was a good boss. Oh, he treated you as an equal.

The farmer stopped the dairying. I just can't remember when that was—maybe about the mid-1960s—but he took over breeding cattle. He kept a couple of cows for milk for his own use, and I was involved in milking them. The byreman was still there because he still had the sucklers and breeders and that to help look after. I was sorry in a way when the dairy was put off. I mean I wasnae really with the breeding cows, I wasn't in much contact with them. When I started the cows were all Ayrshires and he then gradually got one or two Friesians. It just happened to be the kind that he got at the market at that time. The Ayrshires were maybe too dear for the farmer to buy. He had to kind o' watch the pennies at the time. A cow cost a good bit: it was over £100 at one time. But it depended on the sale and that—

it could be anything then from over £100 to about £200 or that. And he had about 36 dairy cows then.

The cows of the dairy herd I knew them all and they knew me. The cows got to know you. I had names for a lot of them. They all had different kind of characters. There were some kind o' wild, others were right docile. There's some would kick you—if you walked by them they would kick at you. But other ones they would let you do anything with them. There was one, well, she was all right when she was chained up but when she calved out in the field they couldn't go near her. Wherever they went to get the calf she started to go for them. It was really natural, mother protecting her calf. But she was docile in the byre, she didnae bother you in the byre.

We had quite a lot of calves at Ravensneuk. We didn't have them all at the one time of course. There were some of them dry at the time—they weren't milking. You put them dry about maybe a couple of month before they were due to calve, to give them a wee rest and that. The calves were turned out to the field if it was summer time but if it was winter they were kept in the byre.

I was involved in calving, though not at nights—the byreman did the night calving. But I was helping if they were calving during the day in the byre. That could be quite a long difficult job sometimes. Of course I was just there to help. I wasnae there to do the actual calving, that was the byreman's job. Normally the byreman and I just managed them but if it was too bad the vet was often called in. With a herd of 36 dairy cows calving happened fairly often. There would be a good few calving maybe at one time, maybe four or five in a week at a time.

The farmer had an Ayrshire bull but after it was put away he got a Hereford bull and then he started to raise

86

the calves for selling and for bullocks and that but he kept the heifers. If he got a good heifer calf he used to keep her for the suckling—to breed off her for the sucklers. And just gradually as the dairy was going down the sucklers were gettin' more and more. That process went on over a number of years.

But the Ayrshire bull calves they were sold, maybe just weeks after they were born. The Hereford ones were kept for maybe a year, to get sold for beef.

Och, well, I think I enjoyed most all of the work I did, just the variety. I had the hens and when Mr Graham senior was alive I had chickens. We had day-old chickens and I mean we had to watch them. Then we had the cockerels for Christmas and New Year. But after the older Mr Graham died his son didn't have the cockerels and then we used to buy in some pullets.

Among all the jobs I did I quite liked the shawing o' turnips. It was always done in the winter time but I didnae really bother wi' the cold—you had a pair o' gloves or mitts on. My hands in the winter time never were really cold because they could stand the cold. I think the job I liked the least would be muckin' the byre! I was always happier when I was outdoors, I preferred being outdoors. I liked the harvest, except when we had to re-stook when it was wet. If the stooks were down and they were damp you had to re-stook them all and you got soaking. Singling turnips is boring but once you get into the knack of it, well. The only thing I didnae like aboot singling was if the weeds were growing up in between the turnips and you settled on a certain turnip you went and ca'ed that one out instead of the one that you wanted. That just came wi' experience. But, oh, the turnip shawing and singling I liked them both.

But I wasnae very keen on the tattie gathering. I quite liked planting them but no' gathering them. It was kind o' sore on the back. And then if there were bad ones you had to fling them out, and you whiles picked up a stone and into the basket.

At Ravensneuk the farmer used to have a contract for potatoes when I started there but I never was really in with that. I might help once or twice if he was short-handed but he always had a gang of women come from Penicuik to gather the potatoes. Up till just before I retired I was helping with the planting but I wasnae helpin' gathering because the farmer is not planting as many potatoes as he used to do—just enough for themselves and maybe one or two customers in Penicuik, but that's all—maybe aboot twenty dreels or so, just a wee corner that was enough to do the farm. Oh, he gives me potatoes for nothing now, not that I need many, ye ken. I just get them as I want them, maybe a pound or two at a time. I could get more if I want them.

When we first came here to Ravensneuk we used to get so many potatoes—I think it would be about ten bags in the year. There was a hundredweight in the bag, so that's half a ton. My father got them and then I just got what potatoes I wanted. If I wanted a stone of potatoes I got them. I didnae have to pay for them. The potatoes were part of my father's wages at that time. And we got milk—part o' our wages as well. We got what milk we wanted really. There was nothing really set, you know—if we needed milk we got the milk, but we didnae pay for it, oh, no.

And then if we got limbs off the trees we sawed them ourselves. Dad used to get a lend o' the tractor and saw the fallen limbs here or saw them wi' the machine up there. We didnae get coals, we bought our own from a contractor in Penicuik. At dinner time I used to just put a firelight on and then surround it wi' wee bits and bank it up wi' big bits and it was a smashin' fire when I came home. So I always had hot water ready at night.

Since I came to Ravensneuk over thirty years ago there's only one other woman—a young girl—that I knew that worked on a farm. She used to work near Ravensneuk at Hall's farm. That was maybe about ten years ago. Of course, Mr Graham used to have a gang of women from Penicuik, as I've said, to work on the potatoes.

There was never any Irishmen working at Ravensneuk and living in a bothy here, no' in my time. One Irishman used to come out from Edinburgh maybe once a year to see if there was a job and if there was a job he got it, but there was no bothy.

The other workers, well, I was working maybe away from where they were working, because I went out later than the men, when they were singling turnips or jobs like that, because I had other things to attend to. I would maybe start at one end of the dreel and they were away at the other end of the dreel. So I was often workin' on my own. I didnae bother. I knew they were in the field but I could just work away at my own pace. I was quite content because if you were working wi' them, well, you had to try and keep up with them, if they were much quicker shawers or singlers than you were. They were men and they had been used to it more than I had. It was hard work at times if I was trying to keep up wi' them so I usually went to another end of the dreel and just worked away and ca'ed off the ends of the dreels for them. But, och, I always got on well with the other farm workers at Ravensneuk. There were nae squabbles, no quabbles at a'.

Well, looking back fifty years since I first started work on farms, there's a lot of changes. I mean, from horses to tractors and from reapers to combines, from single ploughs to three-furrows, and, oh, much more mechanised. There's no stooking now and no binding the stooks together. And then when I began here 35 years ago there was the farmer, the byreman, the ploughman, my father was the shepherd, and myself—five workers – now there's only the farmer and one young man in his early twenties. The old hard labour—it's all gone now. It's easy compared to what it was. At least I think so anyway. I think it's just too easy at times. I think some of the enjoyment has gone out of farm work. But if you like farm work and you put your heart into it, the physical work, well, you can keep fit that way. You've got the hay bales now and the straw bales, and if you're building stacks or building in the shed, you're flinging the bales off the trailers on to the one that's building or up the elevator when it gets too high. You're still doing physical work then. I have done it up until about a couple o' year back when I took ill. And still if they're needing help at Ravensneuk I give them help. I don't ask for payment for it because, I mean, I've got this house. It's a tied cottage. I should be payin' the farmer some rent for this house; so in the sense that he's giving me the house he's still giving me the wage. I just give voluntary when they're needing a hand, and it works both ways because they're good to me and, well, you cannae grumble at anything like that. Oh, I enjoy the work—I'm prepared to do it.

Now I'm hoping to get a Council house that I'm more

or less retired. This house at Ravensneuk doesn't have a bath, just a toilet. I've never been in a house on the farms where there was a bath, no, never. It's always been an inside toilet here, but no bath. So I've always just had a good wash at the sink or else used a hair spray—stand in a basin and have a spray with a hair spray. So that would be one advantage of a Council house—a bath. After fifty years on the farms I still havenae got my own bath!

But I've no regrets about working on the farms. Oh, I daresay I would do the same again if I got the chance.[37]

Notes

1. Hierarchy among the ploughmen is recalled below, page 12, and distinctions among farm workers more generally by J.F. Duncan, in *Rural Scotland during the War* (London, 1926), 194–6.
2. *Lauchter* is defined in *The Concise Scots Dictionary* (Aberdeen, 1985), 351, as "the total number of eggs laid by a fowl in a season".
3. The Union was founded at a conference at Turriff, Aberdeenshire, in June 1912. By the end of that year it was said by its president, Dr G.B. Clark, to have "entered 17 counties, had 80 branches and 5,000 of a membership". By May 1913 there were twelve branches of the Union in Midlothian, including Dalkeith, Gorebridge, Loanhead, Millerhill, Pathhead and Penicuik; and by the outbreak of the Great War in August 1914 the county had sixteen branches, including Heriot and Rosewell. Reduction of working hours by demanding a weekly Saturday half-day was part of the Union's policy from its foundation. But, unlike those recalled by Mrs Tod, by no means all farm workers had won the half-day or shorter hours when the Great War broke out. Two abortive Parliamentary Bills had been introduced by private Members to secure the Saturday half-day, and most Scots farm workers continued to work at least sixty hours a week until 1919, when hours were generally reduced to about fifty. Minutes of Scottish Farm Servants' Union conferences, 9 June and 8 December 1912 (in Mitchell Library, Glasgow); *The Scottish Farm Servant*, Vol.I, No.2, May 1913, 17, and Vol.II, No.16, July 1914, 16; J.F. Duncan, *op. cit.*, 201, 214, 216.

4. Andrew Dodds, a miner's son and a published poet, was secretary of Pathhead branch of the Union in 1912–13, founded Heriot branch in summer 1913, and along with Dr G.B. Clark, J.F. Duncan and several others was elected an Honorary member of the Union in 1916. Journeying 20 or 25 miles a day around Midlothian in his pony and trap on his draper's business, Dodds was in a good position to know at first hand of the working conditions, grievances and hopes of the farm workers. A biographical article in *The Scottish Farm Servant* in October 1913 declared: "A delightful companion, a rare host, Andra is a universal favourite". Dodds was still contributing articles to the Union's journal as late as September 1930. Part of Pathhead and a street in Mayfield, Midlothian, have been named after him. James Rothney, a former railwayman victimised for his trade union activities, was general secretary of the Scottish Farm Servants' Union from its inception until his death in the collision of his motor cycle with a timber wagon near Inverurie in August 1914. Minutes of Executive Committee, Scottish Farm Servants' Union, 11 November 1916; *The Scottish Farm Servant*, Vol.I, No.4, July 1913, 17, No.5, August 1913, 17, No.6, September 1913, 17, No.7, October 1913, 9, and Vol.II, No.18, September 1914, 11.

5. The title was *The Scottish Farm Servant*; it was published from April 1913 to December 1931, soon after which the Union amalgamated into the Transport & General Workers' Union. A complete series is preserved in Aberdeen University Library, and almost complete ones in the National Library of Scotland and Mitchell Library, Glasgow.

6. No more information about this strike has so far been found, and there seem to be no reports of it in the contemporary local or national press.

7. Mrs Tod means bondage and bondagers were things of the past. Bondagers were women—usually wives or relatives—whom farmworkers in south-east Scotland until about the 1860s were obliged by their terms of employment to provide to work on the farm.

8. Pathhead St Mary's Roman Catholic chapel had been founded in 1872.

Notes

9. K.O.S.B.—King's Own Scottish Borderers.

10. Dalkeith Hiring Fair had been held on the last Thursday in February until 1919, when it was postponed to the middle Thursday in March. *Dalkeith Advertiser*, 13 February 1919.

11. *The Concise Scots Dictionary*, *op. cit.*, 116, defines *cornkister* as "a type of song sung at farmworkers' gatherings".

12. *Weekly Scotsman* (Edinburgh, 1860–1967); *Weekly News* (Dundee, 1855 to date); *Daily Record* (Glasgow, 1895 to date); *Edinburgh Evening News* (1873 to date); *People's Friend* (Dundee, 1868 to date); *The Welcome* has not been identified.

13. Mrs Tod seems here to have mistaken the minister's name: Rev. Walter Waddell was minister at Borthwick from 1860 to 1904.

14. I.e., the Union Canal.

15. Mrs Lindsay means that she knew local men who went to the war but none of them were her personal friends.

16. Arles were earnest money—a down-payment on the engagement to work on the farm.

17. *Weekly Journal* (Aberdeen, 1876–1946).

18. Robert Hogg, potato merchant, died in 1959 aged seventy-nine. Since Mrs Landells recorded these recollections Tom Martin's shop in High Street has been replaced by another, Thompson's Sports Centre. The Buck's Head, presently renamed Tropicana, was in Buccleuch Street.

19. The old Kirk is St Nicholas, and Vint's Close ran immediately east of and parallel to Tait Street. The *Dalkeith Advertiser* of 8 July 1920 reported a fire in Vint's Close four days earlier that left seven families homeless. The fire was accidentally caused by an occupant Mary Moffat, or her lodger, smoking in bed. It seems likely that Mary Moffat was Apple Mary. Campend and Sheriffhall lie immediately north-west of Dalkeith, on the A68 to Edinburgh.

20. It may be it was the big hydro-electric scheme at Fort William, north of Glencoe, work on which took place over several years in the 1920s and which included tunnelling, on which Mrs Landells' father was employed. Tackety

boots had round-headed or hob nails or tackets in their soles; sparable boots had small headless wedge-shaped nails there.

21. The fountain was erected, at the junction of High Street and South Street, in 1896 to mark the centenary of the death of Robert Burns, but many years later it was removed for traffic reasons to its present position in King's Park. *News of the World* (London, 1843 to date); *Sunday Post* (Dundee, 1920 to date). Pathhead is 5 miles south-east of Dalkeith, on the A68; Whitecraig, 2¹/2 miles north-east, on the road to Musselburgh; and Gilmerton, 3 miles north-west, on the edge of Edinburgh. The Wicket was a street running parallel with and immediately south-east of High Street. Jarnac Court, presently the main square in Dalkeith, is named after its twin town in the Charente, France.

22. Melville Grange is about 2 miles west of Dalkeith.

23. The Duke of Buccleuch's estate lies on the northern edge of Dalkeith; Millerhill about 2 miles north-west of the town.

24. I.e., a few yards south-east of High Street.

25. The pawn shop remained until demolished along with other buildings in this quarter in the early 1960s.

26. Eskbank lies half a mile or so south-west from the centre of Dalkeith.

27. Dalkeith at one time had as many as eleven registered lodging houses, mainly to house seasonal (many of them Irish) agricultural workers. For many years until they were demolished in the late 1950s or early 1960s, there were three lodging houses in Eskdaill Street: the two, Black's and Reynolds', mentioned by Mrs Landells, and Eskdaill House, the "big" one she refers to, that evidently accommodated about 100 lodgers. *Dalkeith Advertiser*, 2 and 30 May 1907, and information provided by Councillor David Smith.

28. Stent or stint—the space covered in a day's work.

29. At the time of his death in 1959 Robert Hogg's address was 13 Newbattle Road, Eskbank. *Dalkeith Advertiser*, 24 July 1959.

30. In the period to which Mrs Landells refers, there were two cinemas in Buccleuch Street: the Palace was demolished

about 1938 or 1939 and replaced by the Playhouse (now a snooker hall); and the Pavilion (now a bingo hall).

31. Bryans is about 2 miles south-east of Dalkeith.

32. The Masons Arms, 188 High Street.

33. Birkenside, at the south-west edge of Gorebridge and about 5 miles south of Dalkeith on the A7.

34. Woodburn is a large housing estate in Dalkeith; Arniston a village 3 miles south of Dalkeith.

35. Mrs Landells is mistaken about Hogg not employing Irish workers. Other 'Angels' recall that about half-a-dozen Irishmen worked for Hogg during the potato season for many years. D'Arcy estate is about 3 miles south-east of Dalkeith.

36. Edgehead is a village 3 miles south-east of Dalkeith.

37. Soon after she recorded these recollections in the summer of 1987, Mrs Walker was allocated a Council house in Penicuik, where she now lives.